Long Form Short Book

A short book about game of the scene based long-form improv.

Francisco Antillón

Acknowledgments

Special thanks to those who read this, gave me their feedback
and thus made this book possible and readable for human eyes:
Sara de Lille, Gloria Rosario Peña, Alfredo Toledo
Will Hines.

Thanks to my teachers,
in workshops and classes:
Alex Salazar, Angélica Rogel,
Omar Argentino Galván, Piolo Juvera,
Rob Norman, Adam Cawley, Brian James O'Connell,
Chris Scott, Will Hines, Miles Stroth,
Amey Goerlich, Rick Andrews, Sean Taylor,
Brandon Gardner, Rachael Mason, Ross Taylor,
Will Luera, Sarah Claspell, Joel Spence, Kimberly Alu,
Billy Merritt, Sarah Smallwood Parsons,
Julie Brister, Alex Berg, Eugene Cordero,
Martha Stortz, Susan Messing, Danny Avila.

Thanks to my fellow improvisers and teams:
Desayunos Nocturnos, Tobogán, Capitán Gato,
Impro Visa's staff, The Assembly México's
students, teams and staff, We just met,
SBDI, Found in Translation.

Content

2. Creating situations: Initiation and context building
    Concept: Premise
- Initiating organic scenes
    Concept: Who, What, Where
    Concept: Situation
- Initiating premise-based scenes
    Concept: Pulling premises

3. Choosing the game
    Concept: Framing
- Framing within organic scenes
- Framing within premise-based scenes

4. How to play the game: Justifying, heightening, and reloading
- Exploring the game: Justification
    Concept: Justification
- Taking the game to its ultimate consequences: Heightening
    Concept: Heightening
- Reloading the game
    Concept: Reloading the game

5. Supporting the game all the way to the end
- Support moves
    Concept: Walk-on
    Concept: Tag-out
    Concept: Cut-to
    Concept: Split scene
    Concept: Environmental support
- Supporting a scene, ending it

6. Building an improv set
- Unity elements we discover
    Concept: Beat
    Concept: Mapping
    Concept: Connections
    Concept: Callback
    Concept: Theme

Introduction

——————

This whole deal began with the intention of creating a resource for Spanish speaking improvisers to introduce the concept of game of the scene, which is a technique that has grown in popularity around the world.

I played, read, listened, and watched everything I could. I gathered information from all sources and approaches I could have access to, and saturated myself to the point of giving up two chapters in on a previous version of this book.

Then, after a brief pause, I decided to start a podcast: *Long Form Short Pod*. Through this kind of content, easier to write and produce, the goal of contributing to the conversation about game of the scene was achieved - both in English and Spanish.

From the get-go, my objective was to create short, tight episodes filled with relevant information so the podcast would be easier to consume and digest for the audience.

When I realized that this brevity and simplicity were a selling point for the listeners, I returned to the idea of writing the book - this version of it.

A book without the need of incorporating all of the available information, but covering all of the main subjects simply and concisely, using a common language to speak about the game, giving out tools instead of just theory.

That's how Long Form Short Book came to life.

First, I wrote the Spanish version. In Mexico - and Latin America in general - it's short-form first narrative long-form second. Game of the scene is practically non-existent, and I believe it could be, at the very least, a pretty good tool to have in our improviser toolbelt.

Now, with this English version I don't aim to present the definitive resource on the matter (there are many), but to complement those texts by making a short, simple and sweet textbook that goes on about game-based long-form skills and structure.

———

Recently, I took a class with Brian James O'Connell about directing improv. One of the things he asked us to do was to define our voice and express what we believed about improv.

As you embark on reading this, I think it's important to share my philosophy with you, so here it goes:

When all is said and done, Improv is about people on stage making efficient choices and reacting to

efficient choices, with both the choices and the reactions being informed by the inner truth of the improvisers as human beings and the one they discover and explore together as characters no matter how fantastical or absurd it is. You don't need to invent. Everything you need is either inside of you or in front of you.

I know, It's a mouthful.

So what's in this book?

- **Concepts and definitions**.
- **Practical exercises to do by yourself**.
- **A "workbook" section**.
- **A list of reading, listening, and watching materials**.

Also, expect me to drop some names. A lot. Please take this as a way to give credit to tremendous improvisers, coaches, teachers, and authors who deserve it.

I hope you enjoy this book, and that it helps you improvise better comedy scenes.

-     **Francisco Antillón**

"When an improviser has found the game within a scene, (s)he's found the scene"
Del Close, Charna Halpern y Kim "Howard" Johnson
Truth in Comedy
(Parenthetical is mine)

What is long-form improv?

It's the spontaneous creation of scenic moments of which their essence is discovered while they're been acted on stage.

1. It's about making choices

The essence of improv is making choices.

Even before accepting, which lets many go forward as one, there must be a statement or an action to accept. Everything we say and do in front of an audience is a choice.

Can we make "bad" decisions in improv? As a start, let's say no. As long as we make a choice that offers something to our partner and the rest of our troupe or team - as well as to the spectators - we'll be contributing with a foundation to give a solid ground to other moves.

However, it's possible to make *better* decisions. Opting for making our character know what's happening instead of remaining ignorant about it; emotionally reacting to what's happening in the environment or toward another character; and having as much precision as specificity in what we show or say, are better courses of action than the alternative.

> **Choice:** *You're doing something weird.*
> **Better choice:** *I've had it with you offering swedish massages to strangers at the subway station!*

These are better because they help us move forward in our scenes. Executing an action or saying a line that is clear, specific, and matches our character's point of view thrusts us toward what's next instead of having to walk backward to find our motivation.

This is what some of the older "rules" or "guidelines" refer to as "active choices". Don't tell us about the way you are, show it.

Characters are agents of change in the reality we're showing to the audience. They're active entities impacting the moment we are creating right before their eyes, instead of being a victim of circumstance.

Comedy tends to be economical since there isn't room for waste in our words and movements. Everything that happens on stage can be filtered by our character through its point of view and will make them act in consequence.

THREE CHOICES

An example of this is a character like Larry David in *Curb your enthusiasm* or any of the main characters in *Seinfeld*. The most mundane details become the inspiration of 30 minutes of TV because they spark really strong points of view in the cast.

> Will Hines, teacher and author of *How to be the greatest improviser in the world*, speaks of three choices that elevate our scenes: choosing to know, choosing to care, and choosing to say.
>
> Letting your character know instead of depending on others to understand what's going on; making it matter to them enough to have an opinion or feel an emotion; and once they have one of those, making sure your character openly expresses it, will make our scenic choices more important.

The choices we make, besides clear, should be congruous with what we've crafted before. Each word and action are connected and they need to work well together, so the audience can understand which are the "rules" of the scene.

*I'm offering swedish massages to strangers in the subway **AND** my hands are drenched in essential oils **AND** I'm wearing a portable speaker with tibetan singing bowls' sounds.*

The audience needs to comprehend which world they're watching, so they can feel comfortable enough and let themselves be surprised by what's being revealed while our scenic moment is advancing.

Whenever we don't make choices, we're letting other people do it for us. That is problematic for two reasons that complement each other:

- Because we have no control over any aspect of the scene and we'll be inhabiting a situation that isn't precisely appealing to us for that very reason; and

- Because we're forcing someone else to add information to make the scenic action go forward.

Discover and build an instant that is worth playing in front of an audience alongside more people. Make choices.

THE INVISIBLE GIFT

My biggest pet peeve in improv is what I call "the invisible gift".

- **Hi, have you read this?**

A line of dialogue like this one is an example of non-active choices... because there's actually no choice being made there. We're not giving information about the characters, about the context, or our idea. We're just wasting stage time.

You're giving the other person the burden of solving something they didn't create, and by way of that, if you had a specific idea, now it's out of your control and the scene will take its course.

Don't be an invisible gift giver.

BE BOLD

This doesn't mean "be outrageous". It means bring something to the table. Actor and improviser Eugene Cordero says a bold choice is one that puts us somewhere and gives us something to play with.

Also, keep in mind: Improv is an ephemeral art form devoid of any consequences. To quote UCB's and WGIS's teacher, Julie Brister: Dare yourself to make something that makes you feel uncomfortable.

Follow the fear.

Same subject, but shorter:

Dare yourself to make clear choices that make sense with one another. They're all important while advancing the scene.

An exercise to do by yourself:

If you see someone carrying a closed box or package, assume what's inside; and if you see someone doing something that you don't understand, choose a reason behind it. Take into account everything you can see from the person to assume their reality.

2. Yes, And

_____

If you happen to have any notion about improv, you likely know "Yes, and" is one of its core principles.

Concept: "Yes, and"
Accepting something that happened on stage as part of the reality, assimilating it and reacting to it honestly from our character's point of view.

This idea of "Yes, and" has an inner component and an external component.

The internal ("*Yes,*") is the acceptance and assimilation of someone else's offer.

Accepting means taking into account anything that has been already built as part of a scenic truth; while **assimilating** means interpreting it through our point of view.

A way to see this process is: *"This thing that just happened is real within the scene, now I'll use the information at my disposal so I can find its meaning before responding".*

The external element (*"and"*) is the action or dialogue by which we react honestly to the offer, making our contribution to the scene. We embed our truth and our style on what we add.

This exteriorization is what the audience can actually watch and listen to. It's the process that can be summed up as *"This is my reaction to what just happened, since it's scenic truth, according to how I understood it in regard to the context and the characters"*.

Unfolding this concept:

Yes	**,**	**and**
(Internal)	*(Internal)*	*(External)*
I accept the offer as part of the scenic reality.	I assimilate what has been offered.	I contribute to the scenic truth by reacting honestly according to my character, the other characters, or the context.

Understanding "Yes, and" this way, we can take our scenes further, faster. Besides, we'll avoid falling into some bad interpretations that have risen about this principle:

First: "Yes, and" doesn't mean that our character has to say yes to everything, and also doesn't imply we should obey whatever someone else offers. "Saying yes" is an external expression, and an honest answer many times is different than a "yes".

The first part of "Yes, and" is internal, and has to do with our willingness to agree with someone else's offer as an improviser, not as a character.

WHAT THE CHARACTER SAYS, WHAT THE IMPROVISER SAYS

For example, in a two-person scene where "**Stop singing about everything!**" is said angrily, we can assume there's a character whose personality involves... singing about everything, which in turn causes a negative reaction in another character.

> Obeying this instruction **from the character** would make us "disobey" the non-expressed offer **from the improviser**, which is "*I discovered your character makes mine react when you do that, let's play with that*".

This is what the authors of Truth in Comedy (Del Close, Charna Halpern, and Kim "Howard" Johnson) consider to be the only unbreakable rule of improv: "*The rule of agreement*".

Concept: Agreement

An implicit and shared understanding of what is considered as the truth, the facts of the scene.

Accepting the invitation that is made to us sometimes implies opposing the other character, because that's the dynamic that is proposed through the offer.

WHAT'S BEHIND IT?

In long-form improv, and mainly in the game-based variant, finding this subtext is key. We have as a starting point what the character says. But also, what's the goal of the improviser as they said it?

If it has been established that your character doesn't like anything about celebrating a birthday, when

---

someone asks "**Are you excited about blowing the candles?**", the honest answer is "**No**".

Second: "Yes, and" goes beyond accepting offers. When we're only agreeing with everything someone else contributes, we're taking the scene's backseat instead of helping with the drive.

The external element of "Yes, and" is an instruction to be active agents in the process of creation.

Third: It's not enough just adding whatever. Incorporating information disregarding if it is based on what has been previously established as part of the emotional and factual reality or not, is more counterproductive, instead of the opposite.

Let's think about the collaborative construction of the scene as cooking a recipe collectively, one ingredient at a time. We have to take into account the ingredients that have been incorporated before so we don't ruin our dish.

Of course, like in the kitchen, in improv we could experiment and take random ingredients and try to get to a decent result, but that requires more effort, and I insist: Comedy doesn't look for complications, it looks to simplify itself.

When we begin our scene, the stage is filled with infinite possibilities. Each choice we make reduces the number of options until it places us in a situation. If our choices complement each other and are understood as part of a whole, we'll get faster to it.

To finish this subject: Reacting to offers goes even further than adding relevant information. Comedy and improv are nurtured by clear and straightforward points of view.

Providing something to the scene is way more valuable when we add to it an opinion or emotion that makes it an honest and true offer - even when it is absurd. But we'll get to this in the following chapters.

Same subject, but shorter:

Accept what is offered as a fact within the scene, but make a choice from your character's point of view about what that means to them.

An exercise to do by yourself:

Whenever you're watching a sitcom you like and are familiar with via streaming, press pause after a character says or does something in front of someone else. Then, imagine how that character is going to react to what just happened. Unpause and corroborate how close or far you were from guessing correctly.

3. Purposeful attention

Let's focus on what comes immediately after the acceptance part of "Yes, and", but before the response. This is the part in which we decode the words and/or the actions that someone else presented on stage.

The process of assimilating what was offered to us is very important when we're co-creating, and sometimes we don't give it enough time.

Being under the spotlight pushes us to fill the silence between lines of dialogue as quickly as possible. On stage, a pause feels way longer than how the audience perceives it.

Taking that couple of seconds to unveil the content of the offer (It doesn't take much more than that!) starts just after we make *our* contribution. To use a quote from Second City's Rachael Mason: Why go fast when we don't know where we're going?

> **LET SILENCE BE**
>
> To borrow from another really good teacher, Kimberly Alu from The PIT: We don't have to fill every silence with words.

How is our partner receiving our offer? Are they aware of it? When it's our turn to incorporate information, it's also our responsibility to realize if the other person got the message.

THROW A PUPPY

A quote about improv that I think comes from teacher and improviser Christina Gausas says: *"the truth is found in someone else's eyes"*.

Eye contact is a key element to understanding each other in a scene, and it mainly serves as a clear cut indicator of who it is we are addressing our information to, and if that person is getting it or not.

If the counterpart is staring down or miming some action that doesn't allow them to look at you, the probability of your offer not being received is higher than average.

While you send your proposition, think that it's more like throwing a little puppy to someone else and less like throwing trash into a dumpster. You want the other person to catch it - or at least I hope so.

Then, it's our fellow improviser's turn to make a choice and act on it. Right here we should be present to obtain everything that is intended to be transmitted through dialogue and movement.

In several writings, this is called listening. In my case, I like to call it "purposeful attention".

Concept: Purposeful attention

Consciously listening and observing every action that someone else is doing on stage, understanding that everything that is happening is part of the reality that's being created.

When we are present, we take what's verbally expressed by the improviser joining us on stage, but also how they do it and the actions that go with it. As Rachael Mason also says: Our partner is our primary source of creation.

It goes above listening since it implies putting all the attention possible through each one of our senses toward whatever is happening in the scene - be it if we're either acting it or we're part of the team ready to support when necessary.

Think about this kind of attention as the one we use on a first date with someone we really like. We want to know everything about that person, and every single thing they do seems interesting to us. Each little piece of information we get helps us build a deeper relationship... and that's how it goes in improv as well.

Now, if purposeful attention is a tool that can bolster our scenes and give us more interesting roads to pursue at any moment of our improvised scene, one of the most important moments to apply it is at the beginning when we're reacting to an initiation.

Concept: Initiation

The first action and/or first line of dialogue
that is made in the scene.

Whenever someone else initiates, the first thing we should assume is that they have an idea they are looking to develop. It may happen that they started from scratch, but we need to start from a position of considering that the initiator has a concrete proposition.

Thus, our purposeful attention will be directed to obtain each subtlety from the initiation and its evident and subtextual meaning, since that's where the details of our common starting point as a team reside. Being present will always be rewarded with better scenes.

Even when our partner starts without a clue of what they want, purposeful attention can give us a course. By focusing our listening and observation into the most minuscule detail, we'll find meaning in the offer - even when the other person hasn't had a thought about it yet. From there, all it takes is making decisions about it to keep building together.

QUANTUM LEAP YOUR ATTENTION

There was this TV show - quite a long time ago - called *Quantum leap*, where a scientist traveled randomly through time and space, becoming someone different in each episode.

The scientist kept being himself in thoughts and emotions, while the only thing that changed was the body he inhabited.

Then, whenever he appeared it was surprising to him and he had to give himself a moment to understand what was happening, who he was, and how he related to other people in that context, discovering what was expected from him, among other things.

My point here is: Treat purposeful attention like you were quantum leaping. The moment you enter the

---

scene, take mental note of everything that is happening, which will allow you to discover what it is that you have to do - without forgetting your perspective.

Same subject, but shorter:

Listen and observe each detail. Everything that happens counts and is fair game to play, either if that was the intention of the one who made the offer or not.

An exercise to do by yourself:

In a coffee shop, restaurant, or in the street, look at couples or friend groups. Look beyond what they're saying and observe how they do it and how, from time to time, the way they communicate depends on the objectives they have.

4. Reacting honestly

The *"Yes,"* is wrapped between two choices: One that other improviser made, which is what we are accepting; and one that happens after this agreement - it being our own decision about how to build upon what has been offered to us.

As I explained before, it isn't just about any *"and"*. It has to be an element that reflects what has been already incorporated and needs to show a point of view.

Here's where the truth intersects with comedy.

> **COMMITTING TO THE TRUTH IS FUNNY**
>
> As UCB founder Amy Poehler says, improvising means living life on stage. However, some improvisers mistakenly think of truth as routine, drama or tragedy.
>
> Thing is, the truth is funny. One of the main engines of laughter is the relatability that the audience feels with the content of comedy, in regard to their own experiences or common observations.

(By the way, we don't need to make jokes to be funny. In the words of Jason Mantzoukas, **not because an improviser thought of a joke it means the character would**)

Moreover, if we're capable of recreating fantastical, absurd, or other people's truths or fantastical realities and of committing to them as if we were living them in the flesh, that's funny too.

Animated series like *Archer, BoJack Horseman, Tuca, and Bertie* or *Rick and Morty* show us contexts that are foreign to us but are committed to that truth - instead of not taking it seriously.

Concept: Commitment

Living and sustaining the reality our characters inhabit and its singularities, accepting them as part of the ordinary and true for them.

Quoting Michael Delaney, a New York based teacher, speak to the truth of the scene and the funny will follow.

At the beginning of an improvised scene, we're in the business of creating realities. It's where our characters live, they experience it from their perspective and act consequently.

Each character choice takes into account what we have accepted as real - that means, everything that has been offered - and produces an honest reaction to it.

> As Del Close used to say, the smallest, teeniest, weeniest emotional discovery beats the hell out of the biggest one that's phony.

Honesty applies in several aspects: in regard to the reality we're living in, to the relationship we have with other characters, and the point of view of our own.

- Reacting honestly toward the situation acknowledges the elements we've defined as scenic truth about our activity and location. If we're in the wild west, certain expectations come with it; in outer space, there will be others.

This includes environmental and physical circumstances as well as the space and objects we've created through mimicking. Everything we've established as true about our situation needs to be respected by allowing it to elicit a response in ourselves.

I'm on the moon > I do little hops while walking on its surface.

- Reacting truthfully within the relationship we have with another character means supporting our partner by being consistent with the dynamic we have shown.

Sustaining the way we treat each other in a scene is accomplished with each reaction, and helps us decode actions and dialogues from other characters while it informs how ours assimilates them.

In the words of iO, Second City and The Annoyance's Susan Messing: The audience doesn't get angry when you make choices. They do when you drop them.

THE TRIANGLE OF THE SCENE

Author and teacher Paul Vaillancourt came up with a shape to explain character interactions in a scene: the triangle of the scene.

Each side of the triangle has a meaning: What *you* are doing, what *I* am doing, and *what we're doing it about* (our circumstances or situation).

This means the vertex where two sides connect is also an interaction: Me with the environment, me with you, you with the environment.

Three side scenes make for robust entertainment.

- Finally, having our character be congruous about what has been previously offered and what has been attributed to them, makes our choices an active impulse for the scenic creation.

Remaining committed to what we have situationally originated, to the relationship and our character is what complements acceptance and eases the advancement of the scene. We just have to look back and see what we already did!

YOU ARE ENOUGH

A common aphorism that is used frequently in improv since the '80s is "playing to the top of your intelligence".

Concept: Play to the top of your intelligence

Reacting from an honest intellectual and emotional point of view, that starts from our experiences, knowledge and feelings to assume a character or to play a situation with integrity.

Responding with truth to the environment and other characters, and exploring our own, is constructed from the specific point of view that we possess not as improvisers, but as human beings.

We can have a particular style of playing, more or less experience, different formation paths, or a thousand other things that distinguish us from other improvisers, but what makes us unique is our point of view, which is constantly being formed by our experiences.

In improv, you don't need to invent or pre-plan. In the way you see the world, you have a resource that no one else has to carry the scene. You are enough.

I think I have to repeat that.

You are enough.

Same subject, but shorter:

Using your point of view or the one of a character that is different from you, react honestly to whatever is happening on stage.

An exercise to do by yourself:

Going back to TV shows or movies, note how you would react to something weird that is happening on the screen if it happened to you as a person. Observe how your honest reaction could be enough to continue the scene.

5. Creating characters

When we think about memorable characters, what comes to mind is specific and very well defined traits by which we could describe these beings in a few words.

A great example of this is sitcoms like *Modern Family*. From the very first episode, we notice how the characters think and act, which is reinforced episode by episode, season by season.

95% of the time, those characteristics that are widely identifiable don't have anything to do with their physique, but with a deeper dimension that involves each character's personality or point of view, since exploring it in different scenarios and in combination with the traits of the rest of the cast of characters, makes these shows have a long life.

THE MAIN COMEDIC TRAIT

Phil Dunphy is the silly dad who wants to be cool. Claire Dunphy is the controlling mom. Haley Dunphy is the shallow daughter, Alex Dunphy the nerd daughter, and Luke Dunphy the dumb son.

> The way we think of them generates an idea of what they are going to do or what will happen if they share a storyline. Phil and Luke's stories are quite different from Phil and Claire's.

Sure, many times great performances enhance the character and it becomes impossible to imagine them with a different face, voice, or physicality. However, that is just one of their dimensions, which tends to be a physical translation of their personality.

Actors have the advantage of a script and documents that establish the perspective and motivations behind these beings. Then, how do we get there in improv?

My route of choice is the one suggested by Chicago based author and teacher Bill Arnett: starting from the inside out; and this is accomplished by defining our point of view first.

Concept: Point of view

Collection of beliefs, opinions, knowledge, and emotions that become the filter our characters see through to observe their reality.

This set of internal factors assembles itself through the choices we make from our character's standpoint. Choosing to have an opinion or emotion about what's happening in a scene, we show our point of view while, also, we're sculpting it in real time.

Because of this, reacting honestly from our character's perspective is important, and that means being consistent with the offers we have made. As said by UCB founder Ian Roberts, whatever you do is the result of what you've done.

Our character's point of view is a promise we make to the audience and the ensemble of what can be expected from it. Making a decision outside of the boundaries of the expectations is confusing. Focusing the essence of the character through their choices, is satisfying and efficient.

Besides, that would challenge us with a difficulty we don't need: Justifying and building a whole new personality that admits this dissonant trait, and comedy never looks for ways to become harder!

Teacher and author Mick Napier proposes that, before anything happens, we take care of ourselves. Are you going to initiate a scene? Let us know the beliefs of your character or how they're feeling about what's happening. Is your character supporting someone who already initiated the scene? Show where they stand about what has been offered. Bring something along with you to contribute to the reality we're designing.

Once you've found your point of view, it's easier to move it to the realm of the external. A profoundly apathetic person has a physicality, voice, and movements that are different from the ones of an overachiever.

Also, they behave differently.

Concept: Behavior

The voluntary way someone conducts themselves.

Our character's actions must come from an internal will or conviction instead of external factors - which would be considered a circumstance, an accident, or a condition - because that way they become part of a belief and opinion system which is relatable and informs future behavior.

I forgot to take your clothes out of the washing machine
is less interesting and less active than
I just love when you smell of humidity.

Building from the inside out results in a scenic element that helps the scene get to more interesting levels for the audience.

OUTSIDE IN

If we can build from the *inside out*, is it also possible to build from the *outside in*?

Yes.

Those of us who improvise tend to introduce characters very close to ourselves in regard to their physicality; and even though an inside out construction can help us with different nuances, our body could limit the alternatives at hand.

Beginning with clear and specific actions, voices, or physicality, we apply reverse engineering to find out what someone who looks like this thinks, feels, and believes.

Even your environment can inform your character creation process. Second City's Adam Cawley makes a point of establishing that we have at our disposal

---

what's around our character, on our character and in our character. Let's make use of that.

Increase the variety of your characters starting from the outside too, but never forget your point of view as the nucleus that moves them and that we're interested to see.

NAMING CHARACTERS

A lesson in how specificity enhances comedy, is this tip from UCB's Billy Merritt: Naming characters is free comedy.

For some reason, audiences just love very specific names. Also, some names help us define certain traits of personality commonly associated with them.

Same subject, but shorter:

Physical characteristics of a character matter, but their point of view and behavior are even more important for a successful scene.

An exercise to do by yourself:

This is a fun one. Answer an online quiz - like a *Buzzfeed* type - as you would. After that, respond as a character you know, or one that you created. You'll discover more things about them as you answer more tests and quizzes!

6. You, here, now

———————

Contrary to the styles of improv that are focused on the narrative progression of a story, game-based long-form improv directs the audience's attention to what is happening in a specific moment between characters in front of their eyes.

We're looking for more depth than width, by focusing on how the beings we're creating interact with each other without the need to advance a plot.

This spotlight on those improvising on stage occasionally becomes pressure to "do something interesting", which unavoidably translates to inventing something, that tends to be a goal the characters have to achieve later or a character offstage that hasn't even been introduced.

In summary, in those instances feeling the attention of the spectators produces a sensation of wanting to throw said attention elsewhere. Ironically, creating this external diversion, pretending to "invent" something more "interesting", removes all importance of what we are watching in that single moment.

Why am I watching these people who are only talking about what they are going to do after this, or about people I don't know?

When we believe nothing is happening and begin to invent, we're ignoring something essential: the things that are happening already.

> ✗ *We must keep training for the contest*
> *or Boris will beat us again*
> ✓ *Natalya, that smug face tells me that*
> *you believe you're a better skater than me,*
> *am I right?*

The choices we make and the reactions that emerge truthfully from them give us all the information we need to have a successful scene.

Whatever has to happen, is the thing that's already happening. As Kimberly Alu says: you've already planted the seeds; just water them and watch them bloom.

TRUST THE MOMENT

From a very brief workshop I took with the Argentinian improviser Omar Argentino Galván, something that stuck to me was a line that has a ton of depth:

Trust the moment.

The moment is this slice of the character's life that we're presenting to the audience, and if we're doing it, it's because it is a special event for them.

> When we don't feel confident in the worth of this moment, our insecurity leads us to a "snowball" effect of invention after invention. We start looking desperate.
>
> Trusting the moment, we can breathe inside of it and give ourselves the time to consolidate what's happening. Building upon each character's choices with truthfulness and being congruous, we get more interest from the spectators - employing less effort.
>
> As Paul Vaillancourt says: Let the scene be what it is.

In general, and as we'll see later, in long-form improv we start from some source of inspiration that gives us enough so those of us on stage can open a window that allows a relevant moment in our characters' lives to be portrayed.

Nevertheless, even though we have a starting point - and even more if we don't - the best strategy is being here and now: right in the place we're creating for the audience, in the moment we decided to show them.

UCB's and Convoy's Alex Berg makes a very compelling argument about staying here and now with our choices: **the further the things are from being active and present, the harder it will be to emotionally react to them**. And that's the engine of improv.

By setting the scenic action on that precise place and moment, what comes next is focusing on who are the inhabitants of this fragment of reality.

The characters the audience can watch are the center of our improvised universe. It is them who personify the here and now through scenic choices.

In this book, when I've talked about advancing the scene I'm not referring to the progression of some sort of story, but to the profound exploration of what is happening between the characters on stage.

Drifting away from this road leads us into the weeds of a plot, which can take us far, but also gets us lost. When you find yourself stuck in a scene, make it personal. Make your character take anything that your counterpart offers to be directed to itself, and you'll see how your improv flows better.

> ✗ *Well... pick up your stuff, we're going to the arena to participate in the contest.*
> ✓ *Maybe I'd change my face if you could do a double axel at least as any elementary school girl would, Olga.*

The temptation to tell a narrative is big but never forget: It's about you.

THE HEAT AND THE WEIGHT

Probably the most respected improv duo, *T.J. & Dave*, has as a characteristic seal: they don't ask for a suggestion.

Then, when the lights are on there's just both of them, looking at each other for a couple of seconds, figuring out characteristics of the beings they're portraying and their relationship.

For that, they have the concept of "Heat and weight".

The heat refers to the intensity of the relationship between the characters.

> The weight alludes to the density of the situation they're in.
>
> So, even when they don't know what they are to each other or in which circumstance they're existing, they have an idea of how to treat each other from the beginning of the set, and they fill out the unknown details on the go.

As we give ourselves to the present, to build a scenic truth alongside our partner, and to be purposefully attentive, we're open to the opposite of invention: discovery.

Concept: Discovery

The process by which the improvisers find out together what the scene is about.

Everything you need is in front of you and is the person you're improvising with. The process of making choices, expressing, assimilating and reacting has as a result the appearance of something that's either specific, interesting or strange that becomes the scene's *raison d'être*.

An analogy about discovery that is proposed by Keegan-Michael Key, improviser and co-star of the sketch show *Key and Peele*, is that we should think about the beginning of an improv scene as a "close up" on the characters, and little by little the "camera" will be zooming out, revealing the complexity of their relationship. Discover with your partner "while the shot gets wider".

As Billy Merritt says: Make discoveries, not plans.

FOUR PRACTICAL PIECES OF ADVICE TO GET QUICKER TO INTERESTING SCENES

Four tools that allow us getting quicker to the scenic motor, besides the discovery process, are:

- **Committing emotionally to the scene**. Showing and increasing our character's emotions accelerate our arrival to the nucleus of the scene.

- **Don't talk about the thing you're doing**. It's about the relationship and dynamic between characters, and not the activity they're doing. It's more about a "how" than a "what".

- **Start from the middle**. When we start with pleasantries or small talk, it's harder to leave our context and focus on the relationship. Let's show the audience the dynamic we share as fast as possible.

- **Assume instead of asking questions**. Statements imply making a decision and contributing to the scene. Asking, most of the time is burdening someone else with the responsibility of making statements and not supporting the scenic development. Whenever your character has a question, be sure to filter it through its point of view, so they can assume an opinion instead of formulating a question.

Now, this doesn't mean you should force the rhythm of the scene. Discovering is an organic process and, as The Magnet Theater's Rick Andrews says, the less we rush, the faster we find something interesting.

BE PRESENT AS A CHARACTER AND AS AN IMPROVISER

You can have a scene where your character is dealing with the present of their reality, **and still not be right there and in the moment as an improviser**.

The most common way to drift away is judging. Judging your choices or judging someone else's. Even judging the audience's reaction.

Susan Messing says that if you have the time to judge, you're not doing it enough. You're not committing enough. You're not discovering enough. You're not listening enough.

Reinvest in your point of view or behavior instead of questioning it. Accept the truth embedded in the other improviser's character choices.

We have enough judgment offstage. Let's leave it there.

Same subject, but shorter:

When you are present in the moment and with your partner, you're making things happen and discovering the essence of what you're showing to the audience.

An exercise to do by yourself:

Go to a park and sit down to watch and listen to what's happening around you. Trust the moment and you'll realize that when you're present, there are a lot of things going on.

Section 2. The game of the scene

In comedic improv, what we want is to identify in each one of our scenes one motor that simplifies its execution.

I decided to dedicate a special section to the game of the scene to check out briefly what it is before we go through the structure we use to better take advantage of it.

The game of the scene

———————

As Miles Stroth - founder of The Pack Theater - says: if your improvised scene is comedic, it has a game.

As I'm writing this, the notion of "game" has been around for about 40 years since it was widely disseminated; but we could say that it was just then when it was named because this has been a part of comedy since forever.

In particular, game philosophy was born looking a lot like sketch comedy and its structure.

The challenge of developing this concept in improv was ambitious: Adapting a very effective frame of mind as a byproduct of a constant process of writing and editing, to an art form that by definition lacks the time to rewrite and perfect itself.

The results have been mostly positive and currently we could say the game of the scene is one of the most studied and extended long-form improv styles in the world.

THE GAME IS COMEDY TRUTH

Since Del Close put on paper the word "game" - in the book *Truth in Comedy* - and even with the development of the concept carried by his disciples Matt Besser, Amy Poehler, Ian Roberts, and Matt Walsh - founders of the Upright Citizens Brigade that in turn generated their *Comedy Improvisation Manual* - this has been a concept that several schools have denied or criticized as something formulaic.

However, it's really hard to be blind to the effectiveness that this methodology brings since it wasn't just creating a concept out of thin air, but it was the result of observation of how comedy had evolved until that point, instead.

Paraphrasing Brian James O'Connell, the game isn't comedy math, it's comedy truth.

So then, to head right on toward our subject matter, what is the game of the scene?

Concept: Game of the scene

Consistent repetition of a behavior or point of view that improvisers have identified and decided to explore and heighten through their characters.

Dissecting this concept, we find that:

- There's **consistent repetition**, which is what the largest majority of schools call a **pattern**. Just keep doing what you were doing already.

- Said pattern replicates a **specific behavior or point of view**; this is, a conscious and voluntary trait that is part of our character's identity.

- Those improvising the scene noticed the behavior or point of view, and even beyond that, **they chose this to be the foundation of their play**. Game is a choice.

- The game **only exists when it's played**. It isn't enough to identify and decide the particularity we're focusing on; we must also **explore** its nature and **take it as far as possible**.

- **It's played through the characters**. We want the game **to become a dynamic between the people on stage** while they explore and escalate the specific behavior or point of view that was chosen to be pursued. It's an stimulus-response situation.

> - You build little houses with the pistachio
> shells and that drives me mad!
> - When you get like that, I want to make
> you calm by giving you a shell castle.

> ## JUST ONE GAME
>
> A point that needs to be underlined is that when we talk about behavior or point of view, we're just talking about one of them.
>
> Once again, I repeat: Comedy lives better in brevity and economy. Having the focus and all of our energy on a precise point of the environment, relationship or characters, ensures the delivery of a more successful scenic creation, because both the audience and the rest of the team know what it is about - especially if it's a short scene.
>
> In longer scenes, it's valid that after establishing a game we could encounter new details that draw our attention, and in that case, there are two options: Following them and changing the game of our scene or turn them into secondary games that won't eclipse the main one.

Now that we know that the game of the scene comes from a behavior or a point of view, how do we choose which one is the right one?

Just as the British teacher and author Keith Johnstone mentioned, even though he was referring mostly to narrative improv: the audience pays to see routines being broken.

Thus, what we look for in the actions or ways of thinking is that they're unusual.

Concept: Unusual

Way of acting or thinking that deviates from the expectations we associate to the context.

For an action or opinion to be unusual, we need this trait to separate from what we expect of a given "everydayness", which could entail:

- Something weird or absurd.
- Something very specific.
- Something extreme.
- Something that draws our attention.

THE FIRST UNUSUAL THING

UCB states that besides directing our attention to an "unusual thing", we also should pick the *"first unusual thing"*.

This is because when the audience detects a detail that is out of place, they hope we follow that road; and if we ignore it, it will become part of the scene's "normality".

It's common and acceptable that we ignore some of the out of the ordinary stimuli, be it consciously or accidentally.

Still, if we accumulate several pieces of luggage with extraordinary stuff before we focus on one of them, we'll create a world so weird that this way of thinking or conducting ourselves we are choosing to highlight will have a lot of competition. We want to know what's funny as soon as possible.

If you don't play the first quirky thing, make sure it's one of the first ones.

The different combinations of context, character logic, number of characters, and the way they interact, make possible types of games such as the following:

- **Dynamic or relationship games**. These are the ones where the thing that matters is how the characters react to each other.

In this type of games, we can count the **logical character versus absurd character** (including its variants where there's more than one on either side, becoming **group games**), **status games**, where the dominant energy gets inverted within the relationship; and those where **absurd characters share a point of view**, each one carrying the unusuality they both embody to the latter consequences possible.

THE DYNAMICS WE KNOW

When we talk about logical versus absurd dynamics, we can think about Penny during the first couple of seasons of *The Big Bang Theory*, which contrasts with the extreme geekiness and lack of social skills of the four scientists (or the three scientists and the one engineer).

In status games, there's a huge number of examples that takes us all the way back to comedy classics. If the beings created by Chaplin or Lucille Ball existed in the real world, it would be expected from them to be subdued to the privileged or to authority figures; and we all know that their comedy wasn't like that.

At last, talking about an example of a plurality of similar absurd characters we can find Derek and Hansel in *Zoolander*, where they represent superficial and not-smart-at-all models.

- **Character games**. Here, the unusual behavior or point of view dominates the personality of one character; no matter who they interact with, they'll show they're out of the ordinary.

Character games are different from dynamic games in the way they survive even if the interaction is not perfectly replicated. Think of recurring characters on SNL sketches, where their dominant trait is carried through different scenarios.

FISH OUT OF WATER

This type of game is a classic case of "fish out of water". Going back to *The Big Bang Theory*, even within their circle, Sheldon Cooper was a character with actions and a mindframe that were way off base.

> This example allows us to illustrate that even when several characters have a peculiar set of traits - as the rest of the main characters in this sitcom do - it's possible for them to leave them aside for a moment to contrast with a particular character game, moreover if it's one as strong as Sheldon's.

- **Situational games**. In these, we establish alternate realities that clash with the audience's expectations that come from their reality.

Those starring in the scene can be a part of this foreign habitat and follow its rules; or serve as audience surrogates by contrasting with this unusual environment.

In comedy genres, we'd also find parody, satire and even literary or cinematographic genre work.

We can also talk about the **mapping games** here. In these, you apply the "rules" of a situation to another one - for example, the rules of a first date if we apply them to requesting a bank loan.

STUMBLE UPON THE GAME, DON'T SEARCH FOR IT

Much of the resistance against this technique comes from those who have misunderstood it or those who've had deficient teacher guidance of the process of detecting the game.

Phrases like *"Find the game"* o *"Search for the game"* put a heavy load on those who are improvising since they're creating an extra assignment where it shouldn't exist.

The game isn't something you look for. It's something you do.

Instead of digging to find the thing that defies expectations, we just need to walk on a solid reality and stumble upon what's foreign to it when it's done by someone.

Using the basic acceptance, assimilation and honest reaction tools we create a context so clear that anything that doesn't belong there will be noticeable.

The job of the improviser is just to live within the scenic truth until something challenges it. After that, it's just a matter of choosing to play that disrupting element, using the technique we'll review over the next section.

Same subject, but shorter:

**The game is the comedic engine of the scene.
Find out what contrasts with reality and play with it
during the rest of your improvised scene.**

An exercise you can do by yourself:

**Watching a TV show, identify a storyline where the
show is following two or more characters while
they're looking to accomplish some objective.
Observe how the way they're behaving with one
another is constant until the end of the episode.**

Section 3. Game-based long-form

Game-based long-form scenes are portrayed through techniques and structural elements that are present in most of them.

In this part, we'll review how to execute the game of the scene and the fundamentals of a form or set.

1. Inspiration: Suggestion and opening

In most long-form improv shows there's a phase previous to scene work where improvisers get inspiration for their scenes.

When I say "most" I mean that looking for detonators of creativity from third parties - or even from the team - is entirely optional.

If we perform this phase, it should be with a practical purpose only: obtaining information for our scenes.

SUPERFICIAL REASONS FOR HAVING AN INSPIRATION PHASE

Aside from the pragmatic reason of informing our scenes, there are three more or less shallow arguments that have made having an inspiration phase the rule instead of the exception:

- It's a way to give a personal touch to the show. Creative sources of inspiration can become even the reason behind the whole show.

- We assume it makes the audience confident about the fact that we're creating something on the spot. No one has said they are doubting or has asked for it, but as a community we tend to think it's better to have that gimmick.

- It adds an interactive element toward the audience. Once again, we don't know if they want that - or if it even matters at all - but touching base with the attendance is an activity that is frequently seen on improv shows.

These sources of information go from the smallest to the more elaborate.

· Obtaining inspiration: The suggestion

We'll begin talking about an element that's probably the most associated with improv shows: The suggestion.

Concept: Suggestion

Any input provided from a third party to detonate the creativity of the improvisers.

The suggestion may be as general or as specific as the team wants. It all depends on how we acquire it.

Concept: The get

The action by which improvisers obtain triggers or information they need from a third party.

The most common way to get a suggestion is simply asking the audience to yell any word at all. The positive side of this is that it almost guarantees new words each show, although it has its pitfalls:

- Some members of the audience look for "the spotlight" and try to be "funny" giving mainly "obscene" suggestions - "obscene" understood as what a middle school child would think is obscene.

- If there's any event generally affecting our surroundings, suggestions may go that road.

- Fortunately this hasn't happened to me, but the suggestion may be something offensive or discriminatory.

- Since there is an infinite amount of alternatives, spectators could freeze and say nothing, being afraid to say the "wrong" choice.

If we want our audience to make our job easier, we also can make their role in our set a more simple task.

Making focused questions is a way to narrow down the answer pool. Instead of *"We need a word, any word at all..."* let's be more precise: *"We need a word that sparks joy in you"*, *"...a word that describes your day so far"*, *"...the name of your favorite object"*, to name some examples.

This way, those in attendance will have a smaller universe of possibilities, making it easier for them to come up with a suggestion that will drift away from the offensive, obscene or absurd.

Furthermore, there are more benefits when we emotionally charge our questions (for example, *"something you like about your life"* or *"something that is going to happen and you're expecting"*). This encourages the audience to connect with the show and give an answer that is easier to relate to.

Of course, it's possible to go beyond just one word. Asking for whole phrases, fragments of song lyrics, social media accounts, objects that the spectators brought with themselves... Anything is capable of triggering the imagination of the improvisers.

ALL SUGGESTIONS WORK

When we talk about suggestions, everything works. Even the least desirable options - and even the offensive ones - might inspire a scene.

The suggestion is merely that, a proposition. How we are going to use it or what it is going to inspire, depends entirely on the improvisers.

The role of the suggestion to merely activate the imagination. That's why I believe we should honor the suggestion making it part of our process, but not to the extent of incorporating it into the content of our scenes.

Try to take the first word you hear. This reinforces that we're capable enough to take any spark to initiate, and that somehow we're doing it on the spot.

However, when a suggestion is so offensive it denigrates a person or a group, you and your team have the complete authority to ignore it and look for a new one.

Improv, like all the other art forms, must refuse to be a tool of oppression or discrimination.

· Generating inspiration: The opening

If the audience suggestion is "tomato" and the whole show is literally inspired by that, we'll find a thematic throughline but we'll also be limited in our exploration.

We're just asking for a spark, the explosion is our responsibility.

Here's where the second phase of inspiration takes place, if that's what we've decided as a team:

Concept: Opening

Activity by which improvisers process information, getting as a result ideas and premises to be explored throughout the scenes.

The opening, when we have a suggestion, helps us reinterpret it according to one or several points of view, be it from members of the team, or from a guest we invited to do so. When we don't have a suggestion, it's a useful tool to put all the ensemble on a common reference base.

The goals of this process are:

- **Generating enough information for our set**. This is the main goal of the opening. We want to have full ideas and isolated specifics to enhance our scene work.

- **Putting the team on the same page**. By being an open process where we all share information and points of view while we're paying attention, each member of the team shares a common perspective with the others; what Del Close called **"group mind"**.

- **Drawing the audience's attention with a scenically interesting exercise**. The opening is a foreign component to all the other scenic art forms, so making it interesting will help the spectators invest their attention in our process.

DON'T SHOW EFFORT

We need to understand this process has a clear mental nature, since it's the way we instinctively approach a trigger to transform it into different comedic ideas.

Because of that, something we must prevent is making our effort stand out. Effort doesn't look good on stage and is uncomfortable to those who should be having a good time watching us. And we also should be enjoying it!

Heads looking up or down, grimaces and gesticulation that shows nervousness or difficulties, elusive glances... If the spectators notice it, they'll start to lose faith in our improvising skills, instead of being predisposed to have a good time.

T.J. Jagodowski and David Pasquesi, in their book Improvisation at the speed of life, put this very simply: Energy is beautiful; effort is ugly.

Wu wei is a Taoism and Confucianism concept that refers to "effortless action". When we adopt this state, we flow in perfect harmony and economize the energy we put in our activity, making us more efficient.

Let's take into account the opening is part of the whole scenic piece, and as such we should make it look like an entertaining exercise that is worth watching.

Let's make it an effortless use of our energy.

Depending on the kind of opening we're doing, any number of team members can participate; and those who aren't doing it actively - this is, speaking or executing an action - should remain alert to get inspiration that may influence the content of their scenes.

The fact that all of the improvisers on a team give their purposeful attention to what's coming from the opening, guarantees that after the initiation, those who join a scene will have a notion of what is being offered.

Now we'll briefly go through the most utilized openings in long-form shows.

- **Monologue**. In this one, one or several people present to the audience an anecdote or opinion that was triggered by the suggestion.

Depending on the team's previous agreement, the monologue will be in charge of only one, some or all team members. Even more, it's usual that a third person handles the monologue, which could be an audience member or a special guest.

Monologists need to understand that their role is speaking honestly about emotional experiences that transcend the common course of their day, preferably being specific and taking tangents from the main story. A monologue doesn't need to be funny, that's a task for the improvisers.

On the other hand, those who are listening must take a mental note of what they found interesting, specific or weird to use in their scenes. This is what we call **"deconstruction"**.

A version of this opening is the **character monologue**, where improvisers must adopt points of view and physicalities that express, through a perspective created in the moment, what the suggestion detonates for their character.

- **Living room**. The living room has become popular because of its fluid and informal nature, which shows the team member's chemistry with one another.

It consists, just as the monologue, of an improviser expressing a point of view or anecdote inspired by the suggestion; but in this case, the rest of the team is allowed to intervene making comments or questions by which the information broadens.

When the exploration of the anecdote or point of view is exhausted, it can in turn detonate a new individual participation from a cast member.

- **Interview**. Just like the living room, this one is conversational by nature. The difference, in this case, is that the chat is with someone who has been invited to be the subject of the interview by the whole team or some of its members.

It has its advantages and shortcomings: On one side, it allows us to pursue and narrow down information by making more questions, enhancing its usefulness in our scenes; on the other one, the interviewee may be shy or dry in their conversation, and in that hypothesis getting details becomes challenging.

- **Scenepainting or Character painting**. This is a descriptive opening that entails the whole team's collaboration.

What happens within it is that one by one, the team members offer details about a place or a character; the more specific, the better for improvisers since they'll get more information.

"We see a hotel reception, with a large service bell and a guest book".

This is usually done by mimicking and by moving across the stage while building spaces and objects; and, in the case of character painting, other team members take center stage to transform in real time while their physique or personality is being described.

- **Pattern game**. This is one of the classics, that consists of word, dialogue and idea association, and the exploration of concepts with comedic potential.

Those who perform it take turns - in a pre-established order or spontaneously - saying something that the immediately previous word or idea makes them think of.

We must look for personal and emotional associations over logical ones. We're not searching for an association that pursues categories word by word (*red - green - blue*) but something that takes us away from them and leads us to paths we didn't think of following and more complete and specific ideas (*red - blood - passing out in medical school*).

This is because when we find one of them, we can stop associating and start exploring, which refines the information we get and gives us a precise starting point for a scene.

ROOMS AND HALLWAYS

Then, if we had "blinder" as a suggestion, we could play a pattern game like this: *Blinders - The Office - Translating from British - A cockney dictionary.*

Since it's the more specific thing, we'd take *"A cockney dictionary"* as a concept to explore:

A cockney dictionary - Cockney slang mode on Duolingo - Cockney slang UN real time interpreter - Amy Adams on Arrival translating for cockney aliens.

From here, it's possible to go back to our word and ideas association saying a word that was inspired by the last thing that was said.

This is called using "rooms and hallways". We go through "hallways" when we're freely associating, but when we find that interesting "door", we open it and get in that "room".

Depending on how you want to play it, the end of the pattern game happens when it gets back to the original word once or several times; or when enough information has been gathered for the set.

A final note: This opening must be played with a lot of commitment and energy, since its rhythm is less natural than a conversation or a monologue. By doing so, we'll be able to keep the audience in a "watching a show mood".

- **Documentary**. This opening goes hand in hand with the Documentary form, created by Billy Merritt. It's a fairly complex one, involving "interviews" given to "camera", the intervention of a "documentarian" stating the theme and title of the improvised documentary, and a combination of character monologues and a run of both real and fake facts.

In a more concise execution, as taught by Joel Spence, two or three improvisers face toward a "camera" (which could be the audience or another improviser) and act as characters giving a testimonial, which is repeated two more times.

After that, we see another round of three "interviews", with improvisers switching partners and revisiting their characters.

- **Deconstruction**. In most openings, what we do is deconstructing an information source in several pieces of inspiration. However, in this case we're talking about **THE** deconstruction.

In short, this opening plays like a scene. Starting from a suggestion or nothing at all, a couple of team members take center stage and while improvising they offer as many details and specifics as possible, which will inform the rest of the show.

Here, we erase the line between opening and set, which introduces our audience directly to what they expect to see.

- **Invocation**. A way to describe openings is like they are rituals, and in this case that moniker fits perfectly.

The invocation has been less and less used, but it's one of the classic ways to get inspiration.

After getting a suggestion, which most of the time is an object, the cast forms a semicircle as if the suggestion is in the middle.

Then, the group proceeds to address it in four different phases: Describing it, giving objective information; talking with it, as we assign person-like traits; worshiping it, turning it into the object of our romantic or religious adoration; and, at last, becoming it, as we assume the personality of the suggestion.

From the objective description in phase one, the idea is to connect and transform the attributes as we go along, to end up with several dimensions that become specific characters or situations.

The way we end this opening, after becoming *it*, is the repetition of the suggestion by the whole ensemble, saying "*I am* ____".

INVOKING A COOKIE

To make it more clear, let me show you how an invocation would go.

From the one word suggestion "cookie", we'll see three lines for each phase, but take into account that it usually goes farther than that.

This is sweet and it crumbles. **This has** a spicy flavor. **This is** warm and soft.

You are cute and fragile. **You are** spirited. **You are** very comforting.

Thou art the most beautiful and loving being my eyes have ever seen, that I need to protect at all costs. **Thou art** the fire within that fills my life with flavor. **Thou art** the one who eases my pain and sorrow with the sheer warmth of thee.

I am the romantic love and the sweetness of poetry, which crumbles to delight you. **I am** the bringer of excitement. **I am** the world's greatest hugger and I'm here to soothe you.

I am cookie. I am cookie. I am cookie!

As you can see, the traits of the object can evolve throughout the invocation, and little by little offer us valuable specifics for our scenes.

- **Sound and movement**. This is probably the one that has lost more favor from improvisers.

"Sound and movement" is an abstract opening where, inspired by a suggestion or even without it, the whole ensemble begins to move and make noises that mutate along the process.

For this, we use the "follow the follower" tool: whenever an improviser chooses to modify the collective movement and sound, everyone follows suit.

From that, we may take lines of dialogue, sounds, physical postures and situations which will offer a diversity of pieces of inspiration for scenes. Nevertheless, "sound and movement" also has as a weakness the fact that if your team doesn't execute the opening with enough commitment, the audience will notice the lack of synchronicity or comfortableness.

- **Organic opening**. For a long time this opening has been confused with sound and movement, even though it goes way beyond. Contrary to the rest, this one isn't prepared beforehand. Depending on the suggestion, we can mold the shape our source of information takes.

Usually, we also use "follow the follower" for organic openings, and there might be a combination of many set pieces on it. It could be that our suggestion leads us to make "sound and movement", mixed with character monologues and soundpainting.

This list we went through isn't the "ultimate" list. There are an enormous amount of openings in the improv world, as well as adaptations of the ones that already exist that customize the idea generation process.

Moreover, if your team already has a little bit of experience, I suggest you develop your own opening process. You just need an activity from which you can extract as much information as needed to feed all your scenes!

FLOW LOKO AND FOUND IN TRANSLATION

Just to show you a couple of examples of custom made openings, here's a couple I've helped develop:

- **Flow Loko.** This one came up to the mexican clown and improviser Flor Peralta and me while we were designing a duo show. It begins with the improvisers asking for a suggestion based on a conversation they were having right before the show. Then, one of them would do a monologue based off of that, which would be interrupted whenever a mantra-like or aphorism-like line came up.

Then, both improvisers riff on examples of how that mantra / aphorism applies, and then proceed to do some scenes.

- **Found in Translation.** This opening was designed by me and The Assembly Mexico's founder Sara de Lille for an ensemble show, where Spanish speaking improvisers were going to do a set in English.

It begins asking for a specific suggestion: a word in the english language that is silly, whimsical, weird, gross... you get it. After picking the word, the improvisers proceed to translate it to their language, and then do a

---

Google image search - viewable to the audience - and then riff on the results, which in turn inspire scenes.

As you can see, you can mash up opening styles, use technology and adapt to the circumstances of your show. It just needs to provide sufficient inspiration.

FINAL NOTES ABOUT THE INSPIRATION PHASE

- This phase shouldn't last long. At all. It's easy to be entertained by the openings and to keep doing them with the rest of the team. However, as soon as we have enough inspiration, it's a good moment to start doing scene work. Let's remember scenes are the actual product we want them to see.

- The opening has the function of, well, "opening" a set. If your show includes several sets, it's ideal to do more than one. It doesn't need to be at the top of the show; and actually, if your show lasts long, generating more ideas will refresh the scenic inspiration.

- Suggestion and opening don't need to live together. You can have a show without a suggestion, but with a monologue. Or you could have a suggestion and start your scenes right away. You could even dispense with both...

Same subject, but shorter:

> **If you want, take a suggestion, but
> make it your own by reinterpreting it.
> If you wish, use an opening, and pay attention
> to the ideas, details and specifics that will
> enhance your scenes.**

Scene simulator

For this last part of the book, we'll be following some examples from here until the last chapter.

SUGGESTION
"Jamaica".

OPENING
For this example, we'll do a pattern game where we'll go back to the suggestion three times:

(HALLWAY) Jamaica - Bobsled - Subpar Olympic games - (ROOM) - Sad sports mascots - Depressing opening ceremonies - "We can't afford to light the torch, here's a candle" - (BACK TO THE HALLWAY) Romance - Public displays of affection - Subway - (BACK TO THE SUGGESTION) Jamaica...

(HALLWAY, ROUND 2) Mexican beverage - Tequila - "I just can't" - Valley girl - Material girl - Singing girly songs with deep voices - (ROOM) - A trucker dancing a Spice Girls choreography - (with a deep voice) "Shut up, I'm Posh" (BACK TO THE HALLWAY) Typecasting -

Whitewashing - Pearl Harbor - Island - (BACK TO THE SUGGESTION) Jamaica

(HALLWAY, ROUND 3) Aruba - Spring break - Behaving differently in foreign lands - (ROOM) "It's France, we can just destroy things" - "I'd put out the fire, but come on, it's Mykonos" - "We're not married here, Susan, so long!" (BACK TO THE HALLWAY) Single life - Dancing - Reggae festival - (LAST RETURN TO THE SUGGESTION) Jamaica.

In this case, from "Jamaica" we got several comedic ideas to explore, some more defined than others. If you notice, in all of the cases we got away from the original suggestion to resignify it.

In these chapters, let's try having you simulate your own scene.

Take one of these suggestions and write on a piece of paper the most memorable anecdote triggered by one of them, where something out of routine happened:

SUGGESTIONS:
· Vacation.
· Moving day.
· Birthday.
· Date.

2. Creating situations: Initiation and context building

The substantial part of an improv show is the scene work, and depending on whether there is an opening or not, we have two main types of scenes:

- **Organic scenes**. These start without an opening, and they may or may not be preceded by a suggestion.

- **Premise-based scenes**. We're talking about the ones that had an opening from which inspiration was drawn in the form of premises.

Concept: Premise

Comedic idea consistent in a context or reality and a weird, specific or interesting element that shines through. A premise responds to a "What if...?".

Both types are fertile ground to use the game as their engine; nevertheless, the approach for each case is different from the start.

As we saw earlier, the **initiation** is one of the most important components of scene building, being the first choice we make and the one that gives course to the scene we're creating for the audience.

Be it from an organic or a premise-based beginning, a precise, active and convincing initial offer - even if it isn't a verbal one - helps us ensure every scene will be successful.

The main difference between each scene type is that while a start from an opening must offer a context and a weird, specific or notorious component from the initiation - which in turn leads us to start playing right away - in case of an initiation that lacks an inspiration source or those that come from just a suggestion, we have to build that reality and also discovering which is the scenic event that stands out within it.

WHICH ONE IS BETTER?

It's important to underline that there isn't a "better" or a "worse" kind of scene; each one of them offers a different experience for the audience and the improvisers.

Organic scenes are optimal for a more spontaneous scene building and for shared discovery that allows the ensemble to surprise themselves while also doing the same for the audience.

Premise-based scenes are more agile and focused on ideas with comedic potential, so they are very effective from the get-go, and the spectators will become partners in crime with the team as they will have on their minds the premises they want to see on stage

---

from the opening.

When designing an improv show, think about these factors as you decide the ratio of organic to premise-based scenes you're going to use.

· Initiating organic scenes

When our external inspiration - if it exists at all - is just a word or a phrase, it might feel like *we don't have anything*. In the end, there's only an empty stage, and maybe two chairs, with the lighting pointing center stage, making it look intimidating.

With this comes the nervousness expressed as not wanting to be the one initiating the scene, as looking at the floor or by entering a brief paralysis state while the audience awaits.

What happens is that we're afraid of a large amount of freedom, and of showing to the audience what we will do with it.

Instead of "not having anything", we have everything at our disposal. The stage is an empty canvas with no limits for the improviser's imagination.

More than that, besides having an infinite amount of possible situations, we also have a couple of elements that help us explore everything we can do - and one of them is even under our control.

The first thing we have, which is highly valuable, is someone else in front of us. We have someone who will discover what the scene is about simultaneously with us. Our partner is our main source of inspiration as we begin.

And just as we have this person who supports us, we have ourselves and our capability of reacting intellectually or emotionally, in an honest way, to whatever is happening.

In the end, improv is deciding, offering, accepting, assimilating and reacting.

Then, let's see how to use what we have within reach and other tools that result in an effective organic initiation.

First, **choose to begin in the middle of a situation that is happening already**. Starting by welcoming a patient is different from jumping off the moment after they received the news that their tests came negative. We want to engage in the life of a couple of characters when something is going on already, to take that impulse that leads us to find our game.

First lines:
✗ *"Hello, welcome to Houston Warehouses"*
✓ *"I'm sorry, our warehouse policy is not to accept products returned in poor shape"*

The situations are built by "yes-anding" and answering the questions "Who, What and Where".

Concept: Who, What, Where

The main components of a situation, which consist in who we are to each other, what we are doing at the moment, and where we are.

The thing taking place can be materialized answering one, two or all three of these questions that serve as building blocks of what I call a situation, and that other schools call a base reality or context.

Concept: Situation

The instant within the reality the characters inhabit that we decided to show to the audience.

Opening up the window into the character's life while a situation is happening, will always be a firm foundation for the rest of the scene.

Now, given that something is going on, you might as well take the road where **your character cares about that and it makes them react intellectually (an opinion) or emotionally**.

> *"Miss, I find it insulting that you're pretending to return a product this worn out"*

Take inspiration from your own experiences or someone else's, from your point of view and even from what looking at your partner triggers you.

THE FIRST THING THAT POPS UP IN YOUR MIND

Ian Roberts created an exercise called *"flashing"*, which has the goal of us using the first thing that a single

---

word suggestion sparks* on us, connected to our personal experiences.

When we use this technique - or any other one that helps us start our scene from an honest emotional or intellectual point of view - the character we are portraying is already contributing to the scene.

As human beings with life experience, any word can detonate an idea.

* Funny enough, months after writing this paragraph I discovered that Will Luera, from Florida Studio Theatre, calls this instant "the spark". How about that?

Also, remember that you're in this with at least another person, so **your offer is addressed toward someone else**, either if it has anything to do with the relationship between the characters or with the situation.

Showing the other improviser what our character feels or thinks about theirs or the circumstances we share, will give them a launching point for their own offer.

A last useful device is **giving the other character a specific physical, emotional, personal or spiritual trait**. This **endowment** is considered as a "gift" we make to our counterpart since it complements their acting choices.

"You seem to be very satisfied with the
level of damage this product
you're returning has endured"

At this point, we have to point out that our intent behind endowing isn't limiting our partner on their scenic choices. We only want to give them a spark to help them fulfill their potential.

BUILDING TOGETHER, BRICK BY BRICK

I'll ask you to take this set of tools not as a checklist, but as options to enhance your initiation. With time and practice, using these pieces of advice and incorporating them into your technique - as well as developing your own methods - will become second nature.

Also have in mind that the initiation, particularly in organic scenes, has to bring "just a brick" in the building process of a "house" alongside someone else that brings their own.

An initiation that is short, clear and to the point, that shows the truth of your character or of the situation, will be enough to start our discovery of what this moment is about.

From the initiation, that is the first choice that has been made, what's left to do is **"Yes anding"** - accepting what was established as truth, finding how our character feels or thinks about it, and expressing it honestly.

Through this flow of sending and receiving information, we'll gradually define with more clarity our situation, and the more detailed our context, the easier it will become evident something stands out to be used as the entry point for our game.

L.A. based teacher and improviser Craig Cackowski puts it better: Trust comedy will come from improv well done.

· Initiating premise-based scenes

If you have a premise, your first line of action has to be going straight to the point and establishing without a shadow of a doubt at least an element of the situation (who, what, where) as well as the behavior or point of view you want to highlight as peculiar.

> **Premise: Someone who always has to be the center of attention**
> *"Carlos, when you're complaining this much about how much you're having a bad time you do realize my mom is hospitalized here in a coma, right?"*

The big advantage of premise-based scenes is their efficiency in execution - as teacher Amey Goerlich has stated - since having previously generated ideas, all we have to do is play.

But how do we extract the premises from the opening?

The goal isn't to literally reproduce what we got from it, especially if it was a monologue or an interview. We'd be showing the spectators the same thing twice! A premise isn't what is said word by word, but the way we decide to play the point of view or behavior that was interesting to us. This is called pulling premises.

Concept: Pulling premises
Getting specific premises from an opening.

There are many approaches to pull premises, and taking advantage of this variety keeps our sets fresh. Some of them are:

- **Causes / Consequences (Why did this happen? What follows because it happened?)**. Here we want to see what originated the unusual thing, or what resulted from it. This helps us expand our world.

> **Premise: A medical student who's surprised by everything**
> *"Wow! So this is how an open body looks like. How awesome! Nurse, suction. Let's do this surgery."*

- **Character, activity, object, place**. Taking a specific item that the audience noticed in our opening is a good platform, better yet if it's unusual.

- **Analog premise (The same essence, changing specifics)**. This is a new way to keep the comedic idea in a different scenario, adapting to its circumstances.

Premise: A medical student who's surprised by everything

"I can't believe it! There are a lot of cables inside this bomb I have to defuse. Have you seen anything like this?"

CHANGING THE CLOTHES ON THE MANNEQUIN

A vet who hates animals, can be analogically translated into an elementary school teacher who hates children, or a superhero that hates victims.

Our mannequin is "a person who hates those they are

> supposed to protect or take care of", and we're just dressing it up differently to use it as an analog premise.

- **Mannerisms and figures of speech during the opening**. Besides the content of the anecdote or opinion, it's also permissible to use the way it is delivered.

Terminology or slang, intonation, energy, body movements... Everything that happens in the opening is fair game for scenes.

- **Carbon copy**. The easiest resource to play, so it has to be sparingly used. Like I said, acting the thing that was already said is redundant; however, we can take a portion of it and find new ways to carry it without replicating the whole story.

PREMISE AND GAME

It's easy to confuse premise with game. This would be like confusing Lego blocks with the finished result.

The premise is the first part of the game - situation and unusual thing - but the latter doesn't exist until the way it's going to be played is found, and that depends on the reaction it causes in our counterpart.

The game is an interpersonal dynamic which helps us explore the premise.

> **Premise: A medical student who's surprised by everything**
> *Game: A surgeon that's amazed by the insides of a human body **and** a nurse that reacts by being alarmed*

In the case of premise based scenes, **starting in the middle of the action also applies**. After all, if we have not only the situation, but also the strange or interesting element that happens within it, why not show it right away?

When we initiate from premise, **clarity is vital** as well. If we have in our head a clear-cut comedic idea to use from the opening, but we don't make it understandable to our partner, we're at risk of wasting it.

Also, it's very important to **add to our premise an emotional or intellectual point of view**. Instead of just communicating the idea, we're showing how we are already a part of it.

GROUND YOUR PREMISE

Never forget that even when you initiated from premise and defined your comedic idea from the get-go, you also must place it over a context to make it stand out even more.

Even further, as UCB's Sarah Smallwood Parsons taught me, make sure your base reality has stakes that make the unusual even more weird, dangerous, extreme or inappropriate.

We could speak of five types of initiations to start five different scenes from the same comedic idea:

- **I'm unusual, you are normal**. This initiation sets up a character or dynamic game where we assume and personify the peculiar behavior or point of view we are proposing, establishing that our counterpart meets the expectations of the base situation, becoming what we call the **"logical character"**.

> **Premise: A medical student who's surprised by everything**
> *Initiation: "Nurse, don't just stand there, take a picture of me with this kick-ass exposed fracture"*

A BETTER WAY TO PUT IT

In regard to terminology, the traditional denomination for this role is *"straight man"*. However, social connotations of using *"straight"* and *"man"*, could be either discriminatory or not represent who's assuming the part on stage.

The label "logical person" was borrowed from L.A. based teacher Brian James O'Connell, since besides it expresses the idea of what this role is, it's also a more inclusive term.

The job of the logical character is not only to serve as a "voice of reason" within the reality, but also to stoke the fire of the unusual behavior making things worse - as it will be explained when we touch on the subject of heightening - and building a case against the character that embodies that behavior.

- **I'm normal, you are unusual**. Here, we endow one or more people with the specific behavior or point of view that drifts from the ordinary, while we assume the logical person role.

In general, these initiations take the shape of an accusation, a call-out, a confession or the expression of concern or disbelief about the thing that's out of place.

> **Premise: A medical student who's surprised by everything**
> Initiation: "Doctor, I'm somewhat unsettled because you keep gasping while you read my results. Am I okay?"

Either way, we want to let the other improviser know what it is that we're going to play.

MAKE THE OTHER PERSON SUPERMAN

When you have an idea to begin the scene, gifting the other player with the premise may be more efficient than embodying it.

In the words of Billy Merritt, "Make the other person Superman". When you endow the other improviser, the scene can be easier because you are more aware of how to activate the unusual thing.

- **We're both unusual the same way**. Two or more characters share the same behavior or point of view that is unexpected in the situation.

In this case, the initiation has to communicate in a precise way both that the initiator embodies the perspective or action that's uncommon, and also that the other player does as well.

Premise: A medical student who's surprised by everything
Initiation: "I agree, doctor! Blood does look super gross up close."

MANY CHARACTERS, ONE POINT OF VIEW

It's also important not to be confused by thinking that both characters have strange behaviors or ideas that are different from one another. The focus must be singular, and for that we need to start from the same premise and explore it together.

Be that as it may, a scene with two different unusual points of view can be carried as a dynamic based game; even though it could be confusing or complex for the audience, mainly if the improvisers refuse to let go of their absurd perspective for a moment to let someone else's irrational mindset breathe.

- **The world is unusual for both of us**. In this one, we're looking to communicate to our partner that we're in the middle of a situation that is foreign to the logical point of view we share.

When we start this kind of scene, we try to draw the attention of the cast members not currently playing it, since this ludicrous world needs characters, sound effects or scenery to fully play it.

> **Premise: A medical student who's surprised by everything**
> Initiation: "So you also haven't seen a doctor in this hospital that looks like they know what they're doing?"

- **We're part of an alternate reality**. Right here we want to let the rest of the team know that the situation is unusual, but we both are part of it.

Here, the comedic idea expands so much that we build a microcosm ruled by its silly logic.

> **Premise: A medical student who's surprised by everything**
> Initiation: "Alright, let's continue this round of patient visits but I want everyone taking video sharing it to me by the end, OK?"

WHERE DO THE FIVE INITIATIONS COME FROM?

This five initiation idea is mine, but is heavily influenced by the *"position play"* concept that I discovered through its creator, Miles Stroth, and his disciple Brian James O'Connell. It postulates there are mainly 4 specific kinds of scenes.

In my case, what I did was take it a pragmatic step further, and use a classification that, in my perspective, encompasses the dynamics that occur when we play game.

HOW DO I KNOW IF THE ONE WHO INITIATES HAS AN IDEA?

Speaking of Brian James O'Connell, a tool he created to identify if the initiator has an idea or premise or not is "Thing, Concept, Idea".

Behind this theory there's the observation about how, depending on how clear we are about the scene we want to initiate, our body language manifests differently.

If the initiator begins by doing an action, looking at their hands, the most likely thing is that there's no idea prepared.

If they make a statement looking toward the audience, their idea is likely to be incomplete - it's a concept.

At last, if they're looking straight into the eyes of the improviser joining the scene, surely they have an idea in which they want to be joined by someone else.

Same subject, but shorter:

> **The initiation is the roadmap that gives certainty about where we are and where we can go. Make sure the map is understandable, even if you don't have a clear understanding of what your destination is.**

Scene simulator

Now we'll use the comedic ideas we found in the last chapter's simulator to make some initiations.

PREMISE-BASED INITIATIONS

INSPIRATION: CAN'T AFFORD TO LIGHT THE TORCH (INITIATION)

"Listen, I think your frugality as Olympics CEO has gone way too far. Our logo is now just made up of 3 rings?"

Here, we're using an **"I'm normal, you're weird"** initiation, setting up a cheap head of the Olympic committee. We're also seeing the **cause** of these subpar Olympic games.

INSPIRATION: "SHUT UP, I'M POSH" (INITIATION)

"Listen Mad Dog, I own this wing of the prison and I don't respect being mocked because I'm obviously such a Charlotte"

In this case, we make an **analogic pull** from the "biker-spice girl" and take it into "inmate-Sex and the city" from an **"I'm the unusual one"** perspective.

INSPIRATION: "WE'RE NOT MARRIED HERE"
(INITIATION)
"Oh honey, I love you suggested this vacation to Costa Rica to spice up our sex life. Anything goes, rings off!"

Here the initiation calls for **two characters who share an unusual point of view, or even an alternate reality**.

Previous simulations come from the opening, so they're premise-based. This is how an organic initiation would look:

ORGANIC INITIATIONS

(INITIATION)
"I know, right? I didn't think I could pull off braids either, but the whole office has been so chill about it so far!"

We're starting **halfway through a conversation**, with an **emotional point of view** and **directing our offer toward another character**; all this, while **establishing a where**.

Workbook #2

Based on the anecdote from Workbook #1, write an initiation for your premise using each of the five types we reviewed.

3. Choosing the game

Whether we found the singularity that drifts away from the reality we created after an organic initiation, or our premise-based scene presented it from the beginning, it leaves us with the question... How does the unusual look?

Just as we saw before, those things out of the ordinary usually belong to one of four categories:

- **It's weird or absurd**. When we create a situation, we generate certain expectations of *"what goes here and what doesn't"*. The more complete our environmental or relationship reality, the easier something stands out as the opposite of what the audience expects to find in it

When we speak of the absurd, we mean something irrational or something that doesn't make sense within a given reality, which in this case would be a behavior or point of view; therefore, detecting it will be easier when we are present and playing the relationship. The clue for the unusual is right in front of us!

UNITS, OBJECTIVES, AND ACTIONS

A way to approach the absurd is thinking about it through the objectives or desires your character has.

Speaking about theater-specific acting, the legendary Konstantin Stanislavski posits that we can divide a play in "units", within which the characters chase a goal through their actions.

Borrowing this concept and adapting it to this improv subject, we can understand the irrational as the pursuit of a senseless objective using actions that are reasonable for that purpose, or else the chase of a sensible goal by irrational means.

Both the means and the ends can be absurd, but this

Long Form Short Book | Francisco Antillón

> will stand out even more when one of them is rational as opposed to the other ones.

- **It's very specific**. Coming or not from an opening, when a rather specific piece of information exists it usually draws our attention.

MAKE USE OF YOUR SPECIFICS OFTEN

"A CAR"   "A 1984 BEETLE"

In comedy, being specific is a skill so special it contributes both to creating a believable situation, and to break from it.

Realize how you phrase your propositions, and try to make those generic categories (such as "car", "snacks" or "the game") disappear to give way to specific types (like "1998 Ford Focus", "Cool ranch Cheez-its" or "Auburn versus Ole Miss playing for the Tostitos Fiesta Bowl").

Specifics define objects or spaces, but also characters and ways of behavior. "Working in a restaurant" is different from "Being the morning-shift manager in the 42nd and 9th McDonald's".

- **It's extreme**. The opposite side of the unexpected, is when a behavior or point of view according to the "acceptable" parameters within the context happens, but taken to the extreme, which makes it out of place too. It's heightened reality.

It ain't a clueless waiter, it's the most clueless person in human history.

- **It caught our attention**. Maybe this is more subjective. When something arouses our curiosity or interest, it's good to follow our instinct and make it our focus point for a game.

MANY MINDS, MANY VOICES

Having a variety of improvisers on our team, with different "real world" points of view, enhances the way we play.

A pragmatic and relevant aspect of this is that either listening to a monologue from a guest, making an interview, free-associating concepts or yes-anding in the scene, each person has a different sensibility defining and detecting what's unusual.

Some things can be ignored by an individual, but will shine furiously for someone else. Taking advantage of the distinct ways the members of a team see the world will widen our reach to more diverse comedy and audiences.

Either way you go about identifying your unusual thing, make sure you focus on the behavior or point of view that's more active; this is, pick actions, choices and statements over hypotheticals, accidents and chance.

When we use an opening, we find the uncommon element within that process; and when we start from a single word suggestion or from scratch, we'll find it as we embark on the scene.

Even if we took off from two different platforms - organic and premise-based initiations - we're getting closer to the moment where both intersect and start being played the same way.

That instant, is what we call framing the game.

Concept: Framing

The choice of drawing the attention from both the audience and the cast toward something unusual, while generating a dynamic.

The game of the scene, as it's taught in several schools, begins with "finding" the game. This entails a specific action with a focused effort, which is why students and improvisers with little experience are overwhelmed with the burden built on top of developing a context through **"Yes, and"**. As Eugene Cordero says, "it feels so math-y".

This supposed task of "finding the game" also removes an actual responsibility from the players: **Deciding what the game is**.

Remember: **game is a choice**. There can be ten things that challenge the expectations of the reality we're playing in, with different degrees of magnitude and nature; but only after we identify one of them and choose to put it under the spotlight, we'll have a game. It's about making our comedy specific.

That's what framing is all about, and it's an important tool because:

- We're giving certainty to the spectators that something unusual happened and of how it is we're going to react each time it does.

- The path we're following becomes obvious for the ensemble.

- If our counterpart identified the same behavior or point of view as one to highlight, we'll be confirming it; if they didn't, it'll be clarified.

- We're setting up, literally, the rules of the game.

> There's nothing wrong with being clear in front of the audience.

Now, depending on the scene type we're playing and the initiation we made, it'll be the way we're going to frame it:

· Framing within organic scenes

The things we did before reaching the moment of framing were accepting, assimilating and proposing alongside someone else, which revealed a situation.

The more we outline our reality, the easier it is for something unusual to happen. And when we're more mindful of what's going on around us, it becomes more simple to be aware of it.

When something out of the common appears, there are two scenarios:

- **That it was perceived by the one who didn't express the unusual**. This is the most common situation, because when we're truly present during the joint scene building, it's easier to notice the thing that doesn't add up.

After accepting that as a scenic truth, the only thing left is to assimilate how our character feels about it.

An alternative is to become the voice of reason, which implies assuming different attitudes - like anger, annoyance, upsetness, discomfort, confusion, concern, fear, curiosity, among others - while reacting to the thing that goes against expectations. Any chosen alternative to express "something isn't right here" that is congruent with the situation and our character puts us in that role, in which the funniest thing we can do is just keep being "normal" while we help our scene partner to keep being unusual.

Unusual behavior
Enjoying bad news in the newspaper
Some ways to be the voice of reason
"Unbelievable! You're laughing at the accidents again?"
"I always see you giggle when you're reading the crime section. Why is that?"
"I just don't understand why you enjoy reading about other people's pain. Are you ok?"

If that reaction implied assuming the same point of view or behavior and the energy imprinted by the character who originated it, we'd be "sharing the unusual", framing a **peas in a pod, mirroring or matching game**.

"¡Oh! Have you gotten to the part where they talk about job losses? I cried laughing!"

- **That it is detected by the one who expressed the unusual**. In improv, it's great to surprise ourselves. Here, in the immediately posterior moment after our own action or line, we realize the potential it has for a game.

Then, there are two possibilities: That our counterpart realizes that too, and reacts framing; or that this is not the case, and then we have to reinvest in the point of view or behavior doubling down and expressing it again.

Either if they did or didn't become aware of it, the character's reaction will set up a dynamic and, therefore, will frame a game.

TRUST YOUR INSTINCT

Any reaction that feels honest in the moment, according to the situation the characters inhabit and the relationship between them, will be the right one.

We usually have a default setting for framing. In my case, my instinctive option is to assume the role of a logical character that gets increasingly frustrated.

Having a known safe space is fine.

But also, taking risks is incredible. After all, you'll be playing the same game, but from a different vantage point.

· Framing within premise-based scenes

Premise-based scenes are more to the point, since the initiation itself - a good initiation - does 90% of the framing work.

With our initiation we express the situation - completely or partially - along with the element that is foreign to it; even more, in many situations, we'll endow our partner with the way they feel about it.

In addition to those "information-loaded" initiations, there are also some "open" initiations - this means, those that express the premise but don't presuppose the role the other improviser should assume.

We'd be talking, for example, of an "I'm weird" initiation instead of an "I'm weird and you're normal" or "I'm weird and you're weird as well" initiation. We're leaving to the other character the option to assume either position, being that choice the one that frames our interaction.

In the different kinds of premise-based initiations we went through the last chapter, the framing would go as follows:

- **I am unusual, you are normal**. The reaction of the logical person, from concern to anger, simplifies the game to *"when you do this, it makes me react like that"*.

> **Premise:** *What if a funeral home wanted to be more fun?*
> **Initiation:** *"If you look this way, you can see our line of pyrotechnics coffins"*
> **Framing reaction:** *"Im sorry, did I hear correctly? Pyrotechnics coffins?"*

If you leave your initiation open-ended ("I'm weird"), your counterpart has as an alternative to be the voice of reason, sharing your behavior or point of view, or framing that both of you are part of a world where this "weirdness" is the rule instead of the exception.

- **I'm normal, you're unusual**. The character that was endowed with the extraordinary trait may decide how intense does their behavior or point of view manifests itself, and even to make clear to the one who initiated which must be their course to follow (*"yes, I have this particular characteristic, and when I express it I notice that makes you think or feel this way"*).

> **Premise:** *What if a funeral home wanted to be more fun?*
> **Initiation:** *"I don't know if you're getting it. Me and my family are in mourning. Could you please stop it with the maracas?"*
> **Framing reaction:** *"I understand, sir. Should we begin with the conga line then?"*

Once again, if you leave the door open saying just that you're "normal", without endowing a point of view to your counterpart, you give them a blank check so they can assume the role they prefer - even becoming a second voice of reason, transforming your scene into an organic one.

WHENEVER THERE'S AN OPENING, PREMISES HAVE THE UPPER HAND

If you and your team already did an opening, where you got ideas and showed them to the audience, why would you opt for an organic initiation?!

Think about it: The ensemble explored premises for about 5 minutes - which is about 20% of a standard set - putting themselves on the same plane of reference, in a state of tacit agreement. The audience saw this process and even has in mind the scenic possibilities.

The process ends. And the first thing we do is set up a scene that doesn't use a single thing that was examined.

This would result in making our opening a waste of time for the team and the audience.

- **We both are weird**. Here we confirm that we received the initiation by expressing our unusual behavior or point of view with the same energy (or maybe a little bit more).

> **Premise:** *What if a funeral home wanted to be more fun?*
> **Initiation:** *"I'm done preparing Mrs. Davis' body like you said. Do you think the face paint does make her look like Spider-Man?"*
> **Framing reaction:** *"Don't worry, the costume and the harness will do the trick"*

Susan Messing speaks about "protecting the freak". Embracing their point of view and sharing it is the ultimate way to do it.

- **We're both normal visiting a weird world**. Remember this type of scene requires a level of understanding that goes beyond the improvisers taking center stage, it has to get to those who are waiting to support the building of this strange universe.

Just like the initiation has to be very concise, the reaction toward it has to be proportional to the perspective and emotion of the initiator in regard to this foreign context, contributing with data that informs the rest of the cast in their work of drawing the unusual environment that surrounds us.

> **Premise:** *What if a funeral home wanted to be more fun?*
> **Initiation:** *"Laura, I'm very sorry for your loss. So... your dad was a big karaoke guy, or what's happening here?"*

> **Framing reaction:** *"I swear I don't have a clue. I think I even saw a ventriloquist in the chapel"*

- **We're part of an alternate reality**. The initiation should've informed us that we're both part of an alternate universe, with special rules followed by all of us who are inhabiting it.

> **Premise:** *What if a funeral home wanted to be more fun?*
> **Initiation:** *"Hey everyone! The next round of coffin top beer pong starts In five minutes"*
> **Framing reaction:** *"I think the next team was hanging out around the margarita bar, whenever my in memoriam temp tattoo is finished I'll go get them"*

Following this offer is simple: Accepting, assimilating and proposing. Like any improvised reality, its creation is ruled by "Yes, and"; and a way to make it even more tangible is to reinforce its rules and add specifics.

FRAMING THE UNUSUAL, BUT ALSO THE RESPONSE

Summing up, we don't want just to frame a thing that drifts from what's normal, but also the reaction to it. Putting the spotlight on the whole dynamic is showing the game.

> The game's formula is always **unusual + reaction**.

To finish the point about framing, it's important to emphasize: When we start from something we brought from the opening, we only use one premise by scene.

It's tempting for improvisers to use several pieces of information obtained from the opening on a single scene - especially in the one that immediately follows it.

What we cause by using more than one premise is that we'll be spending a great portion of the inspiration for the whole set in just a little section of it.

Besides, juggling several absurd or specific things will confuse the audience, because since we're only framing a game, the rest of the elements are noise.

Trust your initial choice of a premise will work, and the scene will do as well.

OWN YOUR UNUSUAL CHARACTERISTIC

If you initiated by establishing yourself as the unusual person, or you noticed you did something out of the ordinary, you should be consistent about it.

On the other hand, if you were endowed with the unusual characteristic, own it. Say yes and embrace the

---

unusual, even though that wouldn't be a thing you would do in "real life".

Don't be coy about it. As Julie Brister says: the best scenes have a confessional element to them.

MAKE IT MATTER EVEN MORE

To enhance the stakes, if you're a logical person, react to the unusual thing as if it was the first time it happened, or the last time you'll endure it.

This will take your reaction to the next level, either by surprise or by putting your character on their last straw.

Same subject, but shorter:

Frame the unusual thing and the reaction, draw the map for the whole team.

Scene simulator

We already have the initiations of our example scenes, now let's frame the game.

FRAMING PREMISE-BASED INITIATIONS

INSPIRATION: CAN'T AFFORD TO LIGHT THE TORCH (INITIATION)
A: "Listen, I think your frugality as Olympics CEO has gone way too far. Our logo is now just made up of 3 rings?"
(FRAMING)
B: "I know, I'm ashamed of that… but you have to see how this 30 cents cardboard medal turned out!"

In this case, B reacted being both ashamed of their frugality, but excited because they got a good deal on cardboard medals. This shows the kind of relationship between the characters.

INSPIRATION: "SHUT UP, I'M POSH" (INITIATION)
A: "Listen Mad Dog, I own this wing of the prison and I don't respect being mocked because I'm obviously such a Charlotte"
(FRAMING)
B: "I'm sorry, man. I know I should be

terrified by a guy your size, but I can't believe you're that much into Sex and the City"

As the premise was expressed, B reacted as a logical person kind of mocking the unusual character.

INSPIRATION: "WE'RE NOT MARRIED HERE"
(INITIATION)
A: "Oh honey, I love that you suggested this vacation to Costa Rica so we can spice up our sex life. Anything goes, rings off!"
(FRAMING)
B: "Oh baby! I can't wait to not-cheat on you! With several people!"

By accepting the rules of the game instead of highlighting how unusual the point of view is, B frames the game as a mirroring or matching game.

Now, just to make clear how this would work for an organic scene, we're going to use the example from the previous chapter:

FRAMING ORGANIC INITIATIONS

(INITIATION)
A: "I know, right? I didn't think I could pull off braids either, but the whole office has been so chill about it so far!"
B: "Yeah, it totally works for you! Even Mr. Johnson was sort of impressed with that. I'm proud of your bold choices!"

A: "Thanks, man. I know I can count on you for support no matter what"
B: "No problem, Charlie. Just never let go that sense of style"
(FRAMING)
A: (shifts energy) "Now that I think about it, you've been... kind of invested in my style choices for a while, haven't you "

After building the reality, we discovered the emotional context of the characters, and we got to a specific and interesting behavior from B.

Take your favorite initiation from Workbook #2, and offer which line you would use to frame the game.

4. How to play the game: Justifying, heightening, and reloading

---

After framing, regardless of whether we're coming from an organic or a premise-based initiation, the rest of the scene is played the same way.

We have a situation in which our characters are, with an unusual behavior or point of view, and a reaction to it. We began with an empty stage that admits an infinite number of possibilities to unfold, and now we're down to a single comedic dynamic to pursue.

This is what the game of the scene brings to the table as an improv tool: Making our life easier, simplifying the choices that we have to make as improvisers. We stop exploring to begin playing and reacting.

From here, our new destination is to find the root of what's funny, and then take it to its more extreme consequences.

Just as Jill Bernard, founder of HUGE Theater, wrote about the subject: the game doesn't exist until you play it.

> **GO FOR IT**
>
> In the style of improv we're studying in this book, our goal is to *get* to the game so we can *play* the game.
>
> So, once we get to this point, let's follow Eugene Cordero's advice and be aggressively playful with the thing we found funny.
>
> It doesn't matter if you want to hit the game hard and often, or if you want to play it slow. Just go for it.

· Exploring the game: Justification

Once we've established a game, our objective is to play it each time we get a chance, and take it as far as possible.

A common pitfall when game begins to be practiced is that we focus on its "nouns" or specifics instead of the dynamic.

If we have a scene with a butcher who attempts to convince their patrons to become vegan, which in turn makes their client curious, the first instinct is to keep hammering the game, basing it on a butcher, veganism and customer's curiosity. These kinds of games are very shallow, and limited in the reach they might've had.

For that, we want to go beyond what the premise and the reaction are offering us. We want to find what moves our characters to behave in a certain way, so when the moment to advance the scene comes, we go back to it as a **platform** so we can can transfer **that point of view** to more situations where this way of thinking can be activated.

We do this through justification.

Concept: Justification

The rationality that makes the behavior or point of view reasonable to the unusual character and only to that character.

Justification gives us the "why" behind the thing that we find out of place. Even if it doesn't make the audience agree with the unusual point of view, at least it draws them closer to an understanding of why it happens.

When we do something absurd without an apparent reason to support it, we're insane. When we have an internal logic, we're just eccentric.

Humanizing our characters this way invites the spectators to invest their attention in whatever is happening with them. When we lose all dimensions of reality, the ludicrousness takes center stage and the more it does, the more tedious to watch it becomes.

If a person has a reason behind their behavior, it mean they care. And if they care, it's likely the scene will be infused with emotion and commitment, which in turn will draw the audience in.

EARN THE ARRIVAL TO THE ABSURD

Quoting Neil Casey, you can get to crazy town, but you have to take the local.

Begin from "real", and with time - and the tool that follows this section - you'll earn the absurd.

We can understand justification as a philosophy: It's what our character with an absurd behavior or point of view thinks, feels or believes. This allows us to move forward, since a firm set of beliefs influences future conduct.

The way we see things is expansive. It doesn't only exist in the depths of a specific behavior, but also behind all actions and thoughts our character has.

Unusual behavior:
Butcher trying to convince their patrons to become vegan.
Justification (Philosophy): *All oppressive systems must be broken from the inside.*

The unusual thing we discover or incorporate to our premise is the tip of the iceberg. There's much more where that came from.

Improviser and teacher Sarah Claspell explains this with an image that I find very didactic: Having your hand wide open, imagine your fingers are each a behavior. Starting from the tip of your thumb, the first unusual thing, we want to get to the others; however, to get to them we must touch our base first, which in the hand is the palm, and in improv, it's the philosophy or justification.

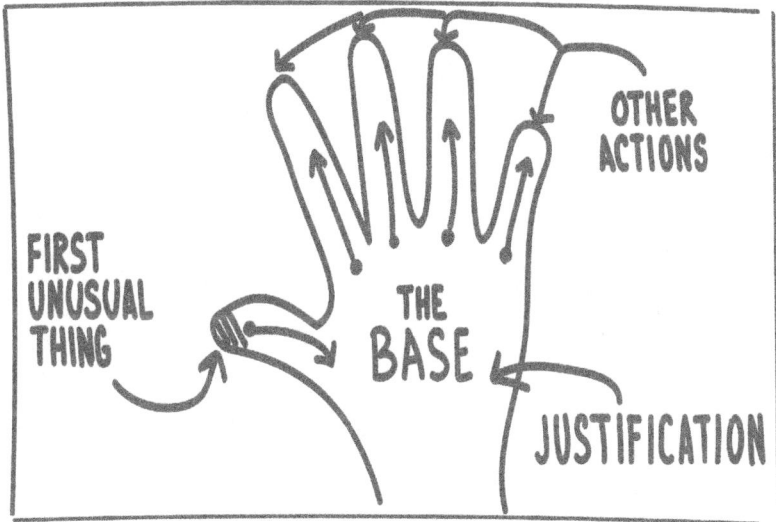

DON'T EXPLAIN AWAY THE FUNNY

The least effective ways to explain the behavior, in terms of improv, are the ones that take away all will, conviction and responsibility from the subject.

An example of this is the character's personal history. Thinking about facts from the past has a little amount of usefulness to explore the unusual, since it makes us look backwards instead of projecting our behavior forward. Philosophy is expansive; history is restrictive.

Other things that are useless for justification are diseases, age, disabilities, being subdued to an authority, made-up facts, accidents, mistakes, force majeure or altered states of conscience.

If the reason behind our point of view or behavior is being drunk or drugged, having a disease like Tourette's syndrome, an order of our boss or being senile, turns what shouldn't be usual in something that is expected from the character. It's practically what anyone would do in that circumstance.

Unusual behavior:
Butcher trying to convince their patrons to become vegan.
Justification (External with no will behind it): *My boss ordered me to do it.*

> We don't want the justification to explain away the funny. We want the justification to ground it, to make it comprehensible despite being an absurd way to act.

The justification tool isn't always necessary when we play. If the behavior or point of view is unusual for being an extreme case of what we already expected, maybe it's just that we're watching a person that raises the volume of the way they manifest it. The reason is clear, the unusual aspect is the intensity.

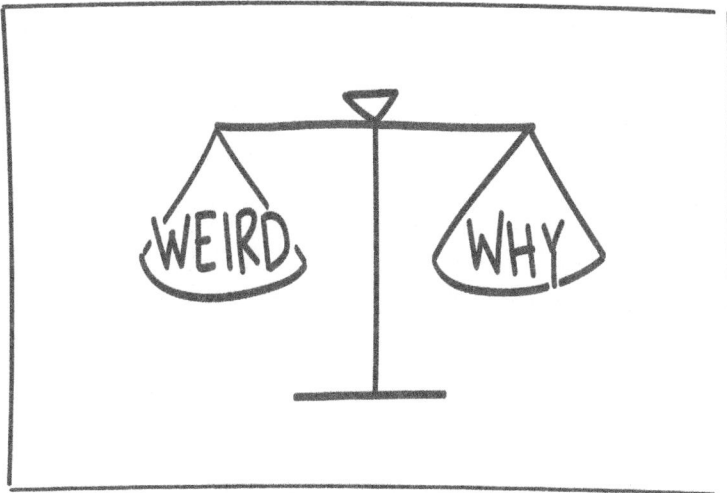

In that same measure, the more strange or absurd our offer, the more necessary the justification, and the more it would have to connect with common aspirations to all human beings so there could be empathy toward the characters by giving integrity to their actions.

THE CRAZY AND THE FOOL

It's 2:30 a.m. of the day I hoped would be the last day of final revisions on this book (by far it wasn't). Before going to bed, I read an article by Will Hines that connected with this subject and a point I wanted to talk about.

I originally wanted to talk about how years ago, when I was studying for a master's degree, I learned that the person that does things without a reason, is a crazy person. When a reason exists, there's space to judge if the action is ethical or practical, but at least there's something behind that's valuable; what philosopher John Finnis calls "basic or pre-moral goods".

The quest for love, friendship, survival, health, personal fulfillment, spiritual well being, the delight found in beauty or the willingness to play... As human beings, these and other pursuits are reasonable, and can make us empathize with someone, even though we don't with the way they conduct themselves.

Back to 2:30: I started reading the Medium post, entitled "Find the fool". I won't tell you about the whole content (Read it. Read everything Will Hines has ever

---

written), but in part it talks about justification as an internal reason in a silly character.

And there's where I felt the connection between the ideas.

The crazy character is the one who has no reason behind their erratic behavior.

The fool might have the same conduct or opinion, but they have an understandable motivation behind it. They're chasing a relatable objective, through irrational methods; or as I heard Ed Helms say, they're convinced of the wrong thing.

No one has ever done anything actually crazy for something like love or survival, but certainly we all have done some silly stuff.

Going back to the butcher example, other possible justifications could be that they want to keep all the meat for themselves, that they're waiting for a client that is the chosen one to deserve their cuts, or that they believe that produce is a more sustainable business. The behavior or point of view may have an infinite amount of justifications, and each one of them ends up as a different game.

When we pick one of those reasons, we get to the launching platform of new expressions for the unusual. It was never about meat, clients or being a butcher. We found the nature of the unusual and we'll be able to serve the game better.

After finding the "why", we'll be able to take the out-of-the-ordinary to its latter and unexpected consequences. Just put it in words to determine which is the guide of your conduct, one that we can go back to so we can reinforce it, and never change it.

> **EXPLORE THE MOTIVATIONS BEHIND THE LOGICAL PERSON AS WELL**
>
> What we're doing here is exploring the whole game, which also includes the reaction to the unusual.
>
> The way a "normal" character acts also has a reason behind it, and getting to know about it will elevate our dynamics since it will inform us of the menu of different ways we can frustrate them, and also will inform the logical character of how to heighten.

Before we finish up this subject, a piece of advice: **The best justifications are personal, simple, broad, specific and discovered, not invented**. The fact that we talk about how having a reason rounds off our games, isn't an invitation to force it. Do the unusual first, find out why later.

To speed up this discovery, imprint an emotional commitment on your character and its behavior or point of view. Just like in real life, experiencing emotions with intensity makes us express our deeper motivations without a filter.

To close our study on justification, and specifically talking about the best opportunity to justify within a scene I leave you with this piece of advice: It's never too late to justify, but the sooner you do it, the more you will be able to explore it.

FLIP YOUR LOGIC

Finding a justification might seem like a difficult task. However, it shouldn't be. We should just react from "the top of our intelligence"; this is, using our own experiences, emotional instincts and snap judgments.

When your character is emotional, they might blurt out a justification for their behavior. Make your commitment to the character a priority.

Another tip, this one from UCB's Brandon Gardner, is this: When questioned about your motivations, start from your own human emotion or opinion, and then flip it (which works as "*I know this sounds crazy, but...*").

FINDING A JUSTIFICATION IS EVERYONE'S JOB

The reason behind the unusual behavior isn't a burden that only the improviser portraying the unusual character should have.

Sure, they have the first shot to express it. But if they don't do it by their own volition, make sure your logical character tries to mine for that justification. Ask them why.

After that, it's entirely acceptable for the logical character to endow that philosophy.

· Taking the game to its ultimate consequences: Heightening

When we are done setting up a situation and framing the unexpected within the context, we discover the comedic truth of the scene. The intention behind having a technique to accelerate our arrival to this point is because we want to spend most of our stage time exploiting it, to squeeze the last drop of comedy juice it may offer.

Thus, we aren't satisfied by identifying something that causes laughter. We want to see how far we can take it.

Concept: Heightening

Making a scene more of what it is, by taking a game
to its ultimate consequences.

When we touched on the concept of game, we
mentioned that it's about forming a pattern of behavior
or points of view, through consistent repetition.

This reiteration, to become more than any other pattern
while turning into the game of the scene, needs to show
us how the unusual is replicated in different
circumstances, or with greater intensities.

Circling around the same specific behavior with an
emotional reaction to it that doesn't increase in intensity,
gets our dynamic stuck and makes it look more like an
argument than a comedic scene with discoveries.

RULE OF THREES

In comedy there's this thing we call the "rule of threes",
which manifests itself in many ways. In improv, it works
like this: If I already saw the dynamic happening in the
same situation three times, it's time to look for a new
way it can occur.

This is because the first time we observe the
unexpected, it strikes us as odd; when it repeats, it

---

gives us a notion or suspicion about what is happening, and the next time a pattern is confirmed. We achieved the maximum expression of comedy efficiency with the minimum effort possible.

After that, the surprise fades away. We need to do something else.

Of course, this isn't a rigid rule, but it's a good tool to think about when it's time to heighten.

Be it from the perspective of the unusual or the logical character, there are several approaches for heightening:

- **If this unusual thing is true, what else is true?**. To its essence, heightening isn't about inventing something; instead, it's about reinvesting in the unusual thing we established, taking it as real, and thinking about what else that implies.

Actually, this heightening option works exactly like "Yes, and" but instead of using it to build a reality, it's employed to accept the absurd as true, assimilate it and offer something congruent with the thing that's being agreed upon.

This way of heightening goes hand in hand with justification, since the latter allows us to go beyond the initial offer to find new ways in which the unusual behavior or point of view presents itself.

Unusual behavior:
Butcher trying to convince their patrons to become vegan.
Justification (Philosophy): *All oppressive systems must be broken from the inside.*
Heightening: *"I'm married for the sixth time because I want to frustrate the most people possible in regard to the institution of marriage".*

The merit of this way of heightening is its gradualness and consistency. This means that, in many occasions, we won't get to the absurd quickly; but the fact that the game is being reaffirmed several times counts as heightening.

HEIGHTENING WITH LAYOVERS

Heightening must be taken step by step since that guarantees a better life for our scene. Getting to the furthest consequences of the game immediately would result, necessarily, in the end of the scene.

In improv and sketch, we call this moment the "point of no return"; however, besides not being able to go back, we can't find an easy way to advance from there.

Taking heightening gradually allows us to further explore the point of view or behavior before we get to that moment.

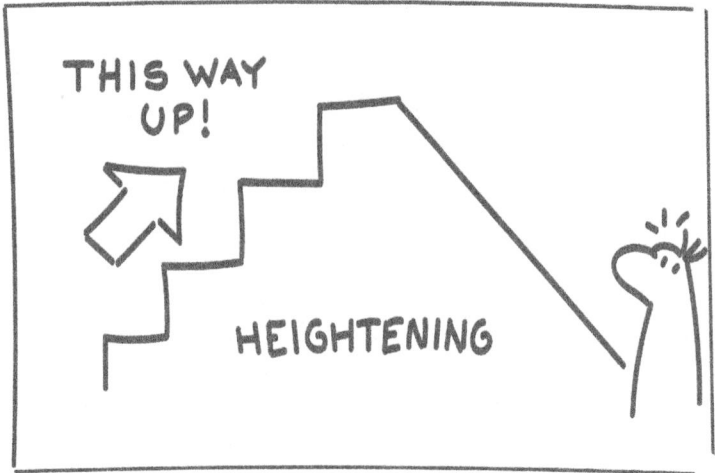

- **Altering the stakes within the circumstances**. There are unusual behaviors and points of view that are more "allowable" in the context of specific situations.

Taking the extraordinary to places where it is more strange, dangerous or inappropriate, will make it stand out more and will generate in the audience a bigger dissonance between what is going on and what was expected to happen.

Unusual behavior:
Butcher trying to convince their patrons to become vegan.
Heightening: *Taking the behavior to a meat industry convention.*

Raising the density of the situation widens the distance between the road of expectations and the one of the unlikely. Yet, abusing of this method can make it predictable, it looks artificial and even incongruous to what we've seen already.

LOWERING THE STAKES CAN ALSO HEIGHTEN THE GAME

There are unusual impulses that, by being extreme, are heightened when we lower the stakes of the situation, instead of raising them.

When someone who's scared about everything is brought to circumstances that get more and more harmless, it will be heightening their point of view by continuing with a fear that becomes incrementally exaggerated.

According to the behavior or point of view, we'll have to tip the scales of circumstances to make them more or less tense so we can enlarge the magnitude of our game.

- **Making things worse**. In game-based long-form improv, we want to go as far away from a solution to the unusual as possible. We want the tension that is caused by the out-of-the-ordinary to not only persist, but to get to the worst consequences imaginable.

In the words of Del Close: We want everyone to suffer correctly.

Unusual behavior:
Butcher trying to convince their patrons to become vegan.
Heightening: *If they can't sell meat, they'll have an excess of cattle and will have to let the cows loose on the streets.*

- **Making the emotion or the unusual bigger and bigger**. "Turning up the volume" of the emotions or of the strange, specific or extreme throughout the scene will reflect on a reaction that also reaches larger dimensions.

Unusual behavior:
Butcher trying to convince their patrons to become vegan.
Heightening: *On their break, the butcher starts a protest outside the store.*

- **Properties, Physique, Personal, Spiritual**. This is a list that I find interesting, that's proposed by The Assembly's Rob Norman in his book *Improvising Now*.

It consists of making the expression of our game take a progression from the mundane to the transcendental.

Unusual behavior:
Butcher trying to convince their patrons to become vegan.
Heightening (Property): *"Try the vegetables instead and I'll give you 200 bucks"*
Heightening (Physical): *"If you don't buy the steak, I'll give you my liver. Is totally healthy"*
Heightening (Personality): *"I'm committing to be your slave if you leave the store right now"*
Heightening (Spirituality): *"This paper is legally binding so you can take away my soul instead of the grounded beef"*

Here, we start directing the unusual to an object, then to the body of our character, then to their personality, and at last to the spiritual, the divine or the cosmic.

This sequence is a step further than the following.

- **Home, Work, Play**. This way of heightening usually leads to "lateral moves" (it means, they don't escalate quickly). Nevertheless, it's an easy course to follow while playing a game.

If the character with the uncommon trait manifests it in either of these three spaces (domestic, workplace or social/leisure activity), it's enough to move it to one of the other two to confirm it.

Unusual behavior:
Butcher trying to convince their patrons to become vegan.
Justification (Philosophy): *All oppressive systems must be broken from the inside.*
Heightening (Work): *On their break, the butcher starts a protest outside of the store.*
Heightening (Home): *Plans their daughter's student council campaign while teaching her about how to bring down the student body government.*
Heightening (Play): *Their soccer team gets to the final, and from the whistle sits in center field protesting.*

Home, Work, Play is somewhat of a classic tool. However, I'd add **Incredible** as an ultimate heightening destination. Go cosmic, spiritual, surreal or fantastic.

- **Widening the status difference**. According to canadian teacher and author Keith Johnstone, status is what we do, independent of our social stratum.

The dissonance between what the audience watches day to day - where there's congruence between cultural, financial, physical or hierarchical "superiority" and our role in a relationship - and what we can show on stage giving the higher status in the dynamic to the one that would be marginated in the "real world", becomes something unusual by definition.

In less evident examples, even among "equals" there are some slight differences in the role we play within an interaction.

Widening the margin of this imbalance, heightens this kind of game.

- **Upsmanship**. In the dynamics where we share the same weird behavior or point of view, the actions of each character are the platform for the other one. It's kind of a competition, although not a contentious rivalry.

Think of the dance-offs that happen on TV shows or movies as a reference. They take the dancing pretty seriously, and they try to one-up the other person and to set the bar higher for them.

As a reaction to the offer, you'll be taking it as a platform to add to the same point of view or behavior a little bit more energy and intensity.

- **Expanding the world**. This option sweeps the rug under what we expect, that is, thinking about the unusual behavior or point of view as an isolated incident; and it makes it something universal, which answers the question: What would happen if everyone in a microcosm, community or the world thought or behaved this way?

All of these styles of heightening, and all of the others that exist today or will exist later, must impact the logical person. If the intensity of the thing that breaks the way they look at the world increases, the reaction to it should proportionally augment.

When the scene has a voice of reason, we need to take them a step before the unbearable. If we're heightening correctly, the next consequence to explore should be the bursting in anger or frustration of the logical character.

Because of that, we also must look to make the relationship strong enough, or establish that the goal being chased by the logical person is so important, that the only option is to tolerate this unusual behavior or point of view.

While you're heightening, ask yourself **where is the love?** What's the reason these characters are together in the first place?

DARE TO LOSE LIKE THE WASHINGTON GENERALS

Our top instinct when we have a difference of opinion with someone else, is wanting to *win*.

This contrasts with what we want to see in improv and comedy in general when a logical and an absurd person aren't in lockstep.

The Harlem Globetrotters are a basketball team that makes tricks, pranks and breaks the rules throughout the entire game. In their tours, they traditionally play against a team that plays by the book: the Washington Generals.

If the Generals complained all the time about the "illegal" things the Globetrotters do - and even worse, if the officials listened to them - they'd probably win. And surely, it would be a sucky show.

When I took the long-form course *A fuego lento* with the Mexican teacher Piolo Juvera, the note he gave me by the end has chased me for years: *Dare to lose*. Even further, dare to lose it all.

Watching a logical person who little by little has nothing left is way better than seeing a scene that gets stuck because they refuse to "get beaten".

(Since we're talking about this workshop, in one of the walls of the next-to-last location of the Impro Visa training center - Piolo's school - there was a quote which is relevant to heightening: Be wrong in new ways.)

IT'S NOT ENOUGH TO TALK ABOUT IT

While heightening, there's always the temptation of talking about past behavior. But we can make it better than that: Do the thing.

Activity, to quote Alex Berg, drives the unusual behavior forward. And that seems a good direction to take, right?

· Reloading the game

As I wrote before, when we hammer down the dynamic constantly the pattern becomes repetitive, predictable and tedious, getting to a point where a certain cadence is generated, marking down our moves' sequence.

Just like our electronic devices, the game of the scene loses energy over time.

To recover it, we have the option to contain our game, so we can bring it back later on a higher level of intensity. I call this reloading.

Concept: Reloading the game

Consciously stopping to play the game of the scene so we can bring it back later in a more effective way.

THE GAME IS STILL THERE, WAITING

The leading term to refer to this tool is "resting the game". However, I'd rather talk about reloading the game, which implies a more active role for the improviser.

> We're not leaving the game behind, just consciously keeping it under covers while we're still aware of it, and we'll play it again in a timely fashion.

Reloading our game of the scene has several advantages to it:

- **Recovering the game's energy**. Giving ourselves time to stop attacking the dynamic in turn gives us a chance to find new ways to play it, freshening up and strengthening the game when we retrieve it.

- **Generating tension and surprise in the audience**. When we have been showing the dynamic non-stop and then we suddenly refrain from that, a tension is generated in the spectator's mind: *Where's the thing that's been happening and when is it going to happen again?*

- **Solidifying the reality around the game**. As we store it, what's left of what we've built is the situation, context or base reality and we can keep on building it.

Our energy and our offers will be directed to who we are, what we are doing and where we are, consolidating and exploring these contextual elements that reinforce the contrast between the situation and the clashing situation or behavior. This, as I learned from The Assembly's founder Martha Stortz, gives more access points to reconnect with the game.

THE SCENE IS A TWO LANE STREET

The scene is a one-way street, with two parallel lanes: situation/reality and game/relationship (which is the dynamic between characters). They're separate things, but they run side by side.

We can use our turn signals and move from one to the other with subtlety, or make a hard turn to switch immediately.

As long as the game has been set up, the improvisers have the freedom to change lanes.

When is the ideal moment to reload? As such, there isn't "one" instant. Nevertheless, we have to consider that we already should've framed the game and heightened it a couple of times. From there, it's a choice for the improvisers, since we have defined a place to come back.

Having a justification behind our game isn't indispensable before we reload it, although that's ideal. Given that the return to the dynamic is basically another heightening move, having a why behind the unusual offers us a wide array of possibilities that allows it to come back in a surprising-yet-congruent way in front of the audience.

And we speak of returning to the game because that's what the scene is about, and not about the situation. The dynamic gets on "standby mode" until we revisit it, it doesn't disappear forcing us to find a new meaning to our scenic creation.

As an audience, as New York based coach and teacher Chris Scott mentions, we love when we expect something, it doesn't happen, and then it does.

Reloading, such as heightening and exploring, is the responsibility of all players. Some techniques to do it are:

- **Returning to the thing we were doing at the top**. This is useful especially in organic scenes, since if we already worked on originating a reality before getting to the thing that breaks it, we have that known field to explore and advance that situation within the logic of the base reality.

In the words of Joel Spence, **get the process going**. The base reality is something that we know how it works and it has a more or less established succession of events. If our reality is a medical check-up and a doctor is interviewing the patient until something unusual happens, we can go back to the next step: The actual physical check-up.

- **Switching energy, status or emotion for the opposite**. Commonly, when we heighten the intensity of the interaction a schism between points of view grows wider and wider. Doing the opposite naturally takes us far from the game while it regains strength.

- **Giving up your point of view**. Whether you're the logical or the absurd character, you always have the tool of **partially** letting go of your behavior or point of view.

Reasons for that could be, for example: sorrow, frustration, a loving, respectful or work-like relationship with the counterpart, ambition, curiosity, needing to accomplish an objective, among others. Remember: **Where is the love?**

Just keep this in mind: In comedy, we don't want to completely abandon our point of view. We'll give up not as convinced, or even reluctantly, and we'll get back to it later.

- **Taking a tangent**. Sometimes within the dynamic we find a subject or word that may detonate a secondary conversation.

Try to give variety to the ways and moments where you reload the game. If you're doing a set, using your whole toolbelt will make your moves less predictable for the audience, increasing the effect they cause when they happen.

How much should the reload last? This is also very subjective. Generally it should last as much as it takes for us to explore what's around the game, endowing the return with the element of surprise. The more time it takes, the more energy our game will bring when it gets back. As Susan Messing says, slow down and "taste your food".

WOW, OF COURSE!

Combining justification, heightening and reloading generates what I like to call **"wow, of course"**, the reaction of the audience which comes from acknowledgment and recognition (*"I know the character enough to know their behavior"*) and from

---

surprise (*"Even then, I didn't expect that would happen this way and in that moment"*).

Playing the game is a balance between the expectations we generate and the surprising way we confirm them.

Same subject, but shorter:

The game exists until it's played. Heighten it, explore it, reload it.

Scene simulator

Let's illustrate how the game is played in one of our sample scenes.

PLAYING THE GAME

INSPIRATION: CAN'T AFFORD TO LIGHT THE TORCH

(INITIATION)
A: "Listen, I think your frugality as Olympics CEO has gone way too far. Our logo is now just made up of 3 rings?"
(FRAMING)
B: "I know, I'm ashamed of that… but you have to see how this 30 cents cardboard medal turned out!"
(EMOTIONAL HEIGHTENING OF A AS THE LOGICAL CHARACTER)
A: "Liz, this is getting out of control. I'm not sure we can do the games this way"
(JUSTIFICATION)
B: "I know I made it hard for you. I'm sorry, Jacques. Really. But I've always believed you can always do more with less"
A: "Of course, being efficient is something we all can agree on, but it got a bit ridiculous"
(POINT OF VIEW HEIGHTENING OF B)
B: "I hear you. Let's see what we can do. Sit down, grab a box"

(EMOTIONAL HEIGHTENING OF A AS THE LOGICAL CHARACTER)

A: "Wait, what? What happened to the chairs?"

B: "We're repurposing them for equipment. They'll make some sturdy hurdles!"

(RELOADING THE GAME, A GIVING UP ON THEIR POINT OF VIEW)

A: (Calming himself down) "OK. OK. This is already happening, so we might as well go with it. We may be able to spin it as a responsible and sustainable practice"

B: "Exactly! We'll be a symbol of relatability for most people on earth. We're on your side!"

A: "Yeah... Yeah! Changing the world 4 years at a time"

(RETURNING TO THE GAME, HEIGHTENING)

B: "Yeah... about that... How do you feel about hosting the games every other 20 years?"

You can notice here, in a really condensed way, how the game of the scene works in practice.

Workbook #4

Starting off the first two lines of your own simulated scene, write three examples of how you could heighten the game with the same characters, and what would be a justification behind it.

5. Supporting the game all the way to the end

The foundation of improv is the two-person scene.

However, when there are more team members in your ensemble and depending on the style and structure you're playing, the rest of the improvisers have to remain alert to support the game when needed. As Adam Cawley says: **even if you're not on the scene, it doesn't mean you're not in the show**.

> **SUPPORTING POSITIONS**
>
> Improvisers that aren't on stage are usually in one of these formations:
>
> - **Backline**. In this one, the team places itself upstage, out of the light, turning toward the audience.
>
> - **Sidelines**. Instead of being the furthest from the audience, ensemble members that are off-scene form two lines to the sides, looking to the center.
>
> In both cases, the attitude that the ensemble must adopt is **being alert**. Distractions or lack of interest will

affect directly the quality of the show... and the spectators will notice that.

If those of us who are part of the team don't seem invested in what's going on in the scene, why should the audience?

By supporting the game I mean **the only ways the rest of the cast should contribute are either exploring or heightening the game, or consolidating the reality**.

Any other intervention that has a different purpose has no place, be it incorporating a new idea or making an inconsequential offer.

· Support moves

Assisting a scene mainly takes the following forms:

Concept: Walk-on

Incorporation of an external player to the dynamic
that is unfolding between characters on stage.

The entrance of a new character may happen because of a request made from the stage or by an improviser's own initiative; and it has to be done boldly and drawing the attention of those who are improvising through an action or line of dialogue that makes clear what the objective of the walk-on is.

Game:
Neighbor A believes their mission in life
is to make the world a more joyful place,
so they're painting neighbor B's house
without their consent.
Walk-on:
Delivery man: "Mrs. Golladay, I'm here
with the golden glitter, and I can assure
you it will stick to outer walls"

A walk-on must be understood as a role that has to last as much as it's enough to support the game. Unless the walk-on character is essential in continuing the dynamic, after fulfilling their role they should make an exit.

If the character is going to remain on stage, they have to take sides: as part of the logic or of the absurd.

GROUP DYNAMICS

If there's a dynamic going on, you are joining one of two points of view; that is, the side of logic or the side of absurd, and this will result in one of three scenarios: One versus the rest (absurd versus many logical - *fish out of water* - or logical versus many absurd - *center and eccentrics*), team versus team (many logical versus many absurd) or everyone sharing a point of view (usually an absurd one, like *peas in a pod*).

Whenever there are two points of view, it should be played just like two characters in a two-person scene, since game of the scene characters *are* points of view.

Concept: Tag-out

Removing a character from a scene, to incorporate another one to interact with the remaining one, taking them to a different situation to play the same game.

The way to execute a tag-out must also be unmistakable for both the improvisers and the audience.

The custom is tapping the shoulder of the improviser that we want to substitute; or, if it's impossible to touch them because we entered from a different side than theirs, occupying their visual space and making a gesture that indicates they must leave.

The main goal of a tag-out is to heighten, so the initiation after it has to be as precise and brief as if it were premise-based - after all, it's just that, following a pre-defined comedic idea. Also, by heightening it specifies what the person doing the tag-out thought the game was, and defines it for the following tags.

Game:
Neighbor A believes their mission in life is to make the world a more joyful place, so they're painting neighbor B's house without their consent.

Tag-out:
(Neighbor B exits) Boss: "Laura, we're in the middle of a tax audit and you're making confetti out of the invoices!"

The new situation that the tag-out brings for the game - if we want it to increase the rhythm of what's happening on stage - must necessarily take less time to be played than the original dynamic. Taking advantage of it already being set up, helps us to only heighten what was happening before.

In a tag-out, we must decide which character we want to take to a different situation. While considering this, those supporting should ask themselves *"Which character would help us take the game the furthest?"*. Be it the one who holds the unusual behavior or point of view (to put them in new circumstances) or the voice of reason (to frustrate them), the choice would be right if it guarantees making our game last longer.

FADE TAG-OUT

A more sophisticated modality that requires practice and team understanding, is the **fade tag-out**.

It entails walking toward the improvisers, pulling gently the one that remains center stage, while blocking the visibility of the other one and expressing your idea.

The improviser who lost focus, must understand that they have stopped being a participant of the scene, and go back to either the backline or the sidelines.

At last, one single game admits the coexistence of several tag-outs, which probably will accelerate the rhythm to a point of no return.

When this happens steadily and quickly, it's called a **tag-out run**.

Concept: Cut-to

Instruction to transfer the dynamic to another situation without replacing those who are playing it.

This transition, which takes its name from a screenwriting technique, can be done from the backline or from sidelines, and it has the goal of making a time dash so we can see the same characters with the base dynamic in a different situation that allows for its heightening.

With the cut-to, just as it needs to happen with the tag-out, **we want to follow the dynamic and not the plot**. Any transition that works toward a different goal will be counterproductive.

Our offer needs to be loaded with information about the situation (who, what, where) and, depending on how much information is needed by the improvisers, it will be more or less necessary that the improviser who made the move joins the scene to support the new setup, be it on the side of the game or the side of the situation.

Game:
Neighbor A believes their mission in life is to make the world a more joyful place, so they're painting neighbor B's house without their consent.

Cut-to:
(From the backline: Cut to the plastic surgeon's office) Neighbor B: "I think that even if you're paying, stretching my smile isn't something I want to do, Laura"

DIRECT RESPONSIBLY

"Cut-to" is a way to direct the improvisers from the backline or the sidelines. This has the value of introducing an external perspective that notices moves that can contribute to the game.

But also, I want you to have in mind that you're part of an ensemble. Having this resource at hand to support the game is positive; abusing it to become directors, can also generate tension between you and your partners.

Use the cut-to sparingly, when it's appropriate and without putting the rest of the cast in situations they don't want to play. Often, try to be part of the situations that you're sending your partners to with this transition.

Make the cut-to that you wish someone offered if you were under the spotlight.

The rest of the support moves are less effective, and should be used less frequently.

Concept: Split scene

A scene that takes focus while pausing the original one, with both taking turns on which one has the focal point.

This scenic convention requires that within the original scene there was mention of a detail that makes this move indispensable for either setting up the reality or to heighten the game.

When those who play the parallel scene enter stage, they must make clear through dialogue that their offer happens just between them, and their stage picture should be on a plane with the same depth, but on the opposite side of the original.

That way, the split scene "takes the light" while the original one is paused, continuing as a frozen image or as a silenced scene.

As with a walk-on, it's advisable that split scenes are only an accessory scene and that they don't compete for attention with the original game.

Concept: Environmental support

Moves that contribute to create an environment surrounding the game.

Those who aren't actively improvising on stage, can participate by making the situation more real or feeding the game using one of several techniques:

- **Scenepainting / lay-ons**. It's the verbal description of an environment or actions that are happening as the game unfolds.

Also taken from screenwriting, this tool allows us to show in the mind of our spectators specific images that are hard to portray.

- **Characters offstage**. Whenever there are characters that are mentioned or are relevant for the dynamic, but don't need to be in sight - or they should be off-stage - those who portray them should do it like an "off-camera voice".

- **Sound effects, scenery, props and animals**. As long as it's done with enough commitment and not as an unrelated joke, assuming the role of animals and objects that are necessary for executing the game is a useful support move.

With that same commitment, another way to intervene is by making essential sound effects.

> **THE BEST SUPPORT MOVE**
>
> Now, I reserved the best support move for last. This is the main move that you have at your disposal that is preferable most of the time.
>
> ### Don't enter the scene.
>
> Sure, there are moments in which taking an active role and joining what's happening works, but giving space to those who are developing the scene so they can explore the context and detect what's foreign to it is a better alternative, as a rule of thumb.
>
> Only support when you have something to contribute to what other people have built.

· Supporting a scene, ending it

A support move that deserves its own section is the one that ends our scene.

Concept: Edit

Action by which the scene is ended, giving way to another one or the end of the show.

Editing is the utmost expression of support to our teammates on stage. Ending a scene in the right moment is the difference between a memorable one and the kind that outlives its welcome.

The improviser's personality tends to be kind and respectful of their partners. However, this can translate to being less decisive while going for an edit.

The trust we have in the improvisers on stage carrying the scene to a good place is a good starting point of an instinct; and when they're having a better rhythm and heightening, besides being their partners, we can become spectators that want to see what else is going to happen.

Now, as I have explained, the game loses energy as time goes by. Even reloading and with tag-outs, we'll get to that point of no return that doesn't have a chance to grow either.

From there, what's next is either an intensity decrease, when our trajectory was the opposite, or else, the void.

The whole team, and not only those taking center stage, are responsible for concluding in the highest point possible, and that's why editing is an important aspect to dominate.

Identifying the right moment to edit is an art. Amy Poehler, mentioned that if we felt it was time to edit, we should've done it many seconds before.

Educating our instinct of editing as improvisers is something we develop over time and practice. A widely observed rule is to edit after a big laugh from the audience. In spite of the fact that this means they're enjoying the scene, it's better to leave them wanting more instead of disappointing them because we can't take the game further along.

KILL SOMETHING WONDERFUL

Talking about editing, Del Close encouraged his students to have the courage to kill something wonderful.

In front of competitive sports-like improv, that is so prevailing in Mexico and Latin America, game-based long-form improv has the slight disadvantage of not having a clock to mark the end of our scene.

However, the other side of that coin presents a bigger reward: Instead of rushing to find a blackout line, it's in our hands to finish in a moment of success.

In an opposite pole, when time has passed and the scene hasn't advanced or heightened enough to a comedic moment, editing is a relief to those who are playing it.

They also notice when something isn't working, so going from one thing to the other, far from being a grievance, is the best we can offer them.

Closing this subject, another ideal opportunity where an edit is tacitly asked for is when one of the characters changes their point of view. Given that in game technique this isn't what we're looking for, when one of these beings transforms its worldview, it's time to put an end to the scene.

The most common editing techniques should be executed sharply, leaving no doubt to the cast that the scene ended; and they are:

- **Sweep edit**. The most widely accepted in the world of improv, consists of a team member running from the backline or sideline and across downstage. This serves as some sort of curtain, that is visible both for the audience and the improvisers.

EDIT LIKE A NINJA

The one who edits must literally run to sweep the scene, keeping their eyes looking across the stage.

We're not looking to be protagonists, and it isn't a space to shine by ourselves and even less to judge the work made by gesturing toward the audience.

Billy Merritt has the theory that there are improviser skills that fall into one of three categories: pirate, robot and ninja.

When we edit, we're like ninjas: Precise, merciless and no one should notice we're there.

- **Fade edit**. Like in fade tag-outs, the intention is that the new scene starts by blocking the visibility of the last one.

Also, just like in split scenes, new characters have to make clear with their verbal and physical initiation that we're now showing a different situation.

- **Editing by a pre-established signal**. Yelling "Scene" or "Edit", clapping or the whole ensemble making a collective sound is enough to end a scene when there's a preview agreement about that.

- **Editing by opening**. From a monologue to an interview or a structured or abstract dynamic, starting decisively an opening downstage serves as an ending to a scene - and, usually, to a set.

This also replenishes the team's inspiration.

- **Editing by scenepainting**. If the team agrees on it, describing the situation that will be explored in the following scene will end the current one.

- **Tech edits**. Besides improvisers, lighting or sound technicians can edit by dimming the lights or playing videos, sound or music.

These professionals need to have improv knowledge or be assisted by someone who does, so they can find the right time to execute their edit.

THE ONE WHO EDITS SHOULD START THE NEW SCENE?

There are opposing schools of thought on the subject of whether the person who edits should initiate the new scene or not.

Those in favor mention that not doing it means irresponsibility that could result in leaving the stage empty while someone else has to start with their idea - if there's a cast member who even has one.

Those against, affirm that waiting to have an idea means losing an ideal editing point that the original scene sets up, which affects the quality of the piece and, therefore, the one of the whole show

Both postures have some reason behind them, and being aware of these weaknesses allows the edition to be carried successfully.

Same subject, but shorter:

If you're out of the scene, your only job is to pay attention to it to support it in context or game.

Scene simulator

In the example we're following, we'll explore the ways it could be supported through some of the tools we reviewed in this chapter starting from an already heightened moment, that would be ideal for support players to participate.

SUPPORTING THE GAME

(B'S HEIGHTENING MOVE)
B: **"We're repurposing them for equipment. They'll make some sturdy hurdles!"**

(OPTION 1: WALK-ON)
C: **(Entering stage) "Mrs. Chairwoman, here's the prototype for the painted flame Olympic torch. It almost looks real!"**

(OPTION 2: TAG-OUT)
C: **(Touching A's shoulder, they leave the scene) "Are you sure I only need this half-empty oxygen tank to deep dive, mom?"**

(OPTION 3: CUT-TO)
C: **(Loud from outside) "Cut to Liz bargaining with street musicians for the opening ceremony"**

(OPTION 4: SPLIT SCENE)
C: (Entering stage alongside D, whom they address) "I'm not sure that's regulation size, coach"
D: "At least we're not doing pole vault with a broom like Jeff over there"

(OPTION 5: ENVIRONMENTAL SUPPORT)
C: (Yelling from outside) "OK guys, it's time to rehearse humming the generic anthem"

In all cases, the moves heighten the game by building up B's behavior.

Workbook #5

Write an example of each support move for your simulated scene, and decide which one of them would've taken the game to a higher point. That should be your edit point.

6. Building an improv set

———

Through the last 4 chapters we observed how a game-based long-form improv scene works, from initiation to edition.

When we gather several of them, we create a set; and as much as we're designing a structure or a way the scenes interconnect with each other, we'll give a more satisfactory form for those watching our performance.

Human beings enjoy when things make sense. Even though our scenes are very funny being unrelated, infusing a couple of elements that make our set feel like a whole piece will elevate them to a scenic product that is even more of a pleasure to watch.

> **RESPECT THE AUDIENCE AND THE STAGE**
>
> Our art form is, by definition, more spontaneous and informal than others. However, respecting the stage and our spectators is a goal we shouldn't take for granted.
>
> Most of the time, we put a price on our tickets. The audience also uses another valuable resource for them - their time - to invest it by attending our show. And

> we're competing with other forms of entertainment that more or less offer added value to their show.
>
> Having standards in production values and content is a responsibility that when being assumed will also be rewarded with attendance and word of mouth about our show.

These cohesive elements may be discovered as we play, or pre-established.

· Unity elements we discover

Throughout our scenes, we'll find ways to link some or all of them by using several tools.

A way to do this is to continue the game that happened a while back.

Concept: Beat

Unit in which we divide the exploration and heightening of a single game throughout several non-consecutive scenes.

The first time the game appears, it's considered as a **"first beat"**. In this one, we establish the rules that surround the dynamic: What's the reality and the unusual behavior or point of view, the type of reaction it springs, the reason behind it and some other ways this uncommon way of conducting oneself happens.

When we make all of this clear in the first beat and the scene is edited on a high point, another cast member could have an idea about how to keep heightening the game. Here's where the **second beats** appear.

In functional terms, second beats work just as a **tag-out**, with the exception that there are other scenes in between the first and the second beats with different dynamics. The thing we're looking for by revisiting the game is to keep heightening, if we left this possibility open.

SAVE THAT TAG-OUT FOR LATER

We always want to take the game to its ultimate consequences during the scene. There is, however, the possibility that thanks to an early edit or a spark of inspiration we'll find new ways to take it even further.

When this happens, a second beat is desirable and the audience will love to go back to that dynamic, just as it happens when we **reload**.

A note I like to give about editing and second beats is the following: If you've already heightened the game a couple of times, there have been at least two or three

> tag-outs and you have one more in your "pocket", save it for later and edit instead.
>
> Afterward, you'll be able to recover that game creating a second beat with that premise, and the spectators will enjoy it as much for recognizing something that they already know how it works, as they will for the heightening that came from your offer.

There are different ideas about how to play second beats, for example:

- **Time dash**. Maybe the most used way and the one that is more storied within improv, allegedly introduced to Del Close by Charna Halpern.

It consists of transporting one or more characters from the first beat and their dynamic to another situation. I insist, because it could be confusing, we want to follow the game **and not the plot**. It's about the funny part, not about the consequences of the previous beat.

First beat:
A swimming instructor for children who constantly instills fear in their students so they are prepared for everything.

✓ Second beat (following the game):
*The instructor fakes their mother's death
in front of their sister, so she can be
prepared in case that happens.*
✗ Second beat (following story):
*The instructor is being fired for
frightening their students.*

When we bring back all of the original characters, what we want is to recreate their dynamic in new circumstances; if it's only one, we want them to offer their logic or absurdity in front of a stimulus that will result in heightening it. As Brandon Gardner says: Just answer these questions: who was absurd, what was funny about them, and where can we take them next.

TIME DASH (SAME CHARACTERS)

FIRST BEAT / SECOND BEAT

CLASH OF CONTEXT OR VICTIM GAME

Retrieving the one who owns the extraordinary point of view or behavior with a time dash means putting them in a new circumstance where they'll clash with the new context.

A second beat with a time dash that calls for the logical person, becomes a "**victim game**", where we want to take them to another situation that will make their frustration grow in front of the same type of behavior or point of view from the first beat, even though the characters that manifest it are different.

- **Expanding the world**. With this option we want to heighten the unusual to the furthest step available, which would mean that the game became so "contagious" that it's now shared by several characters in the same context.

The scenes that come from an expanded world usually are **mirroring or matching scenes**, which implies that everyone possesses the same way to see the world and behave in it.

> ### First beat:
> *A swimming instructor for children who constantly instills fear in their students so they are prepared for everything.*
> ### Second beat (expanding the world):
> *A convention for teachers who prepare their pupils in very extreme ways.*

An interesting combination of world expansion and time dash is that we take a logical character to a new situation, where the game has expanded so much they're the only one with their perspective.

- **Exploring the justification**. Trying this exploration when a justification was made during the first beat means leaving behind specific actions and directly answering the question *What else is true when this reason behind the absurd is true?*

First beat:
A swimming instructor for children who constantly instills fear in their students so they are prepared for everything.
Second beat (exploring the justification):
The instructor takes their students to family court so they can see how divorces happen, to make sure they can be ready if it came to that.

In case the justification wasn't expressed in the previous beat, we can use our second one to find it.

- **Analogous games**. When we take the spirit of a dynamic that was seen before, but in a context and with characters that are totally different (although they could be played by the same people), we're in the presence of an analogous game.

We're using the same mannequin, to dress it up in another way.

Let's say in our first beat we had the scene about the swimming instructor scaring their pupils. An analogous second round would transport the essence of a person who prepares those they're taking care of in extreme ways to a new "Who, What, Where".

Thus, a mother teaching her son to drive or a funeral home makeup artist teaching their apprentice could replicate what happened in the first beat, with new specifics according to the context, like *"Sometimes people are small or they're ducking and you wouldn't realize you ran them over"* or *"I guess if you do a good work fixing her face she won't wake up to attack you"*.

MAPPING TECHNIQUE

To successfully carry this kind of second beats, we use the mapping technique that we lightly touched on in another chapter.

Concept: Mapping

Using the rules of a game or situation, taking them to another one.

We could say mapping technique answers to the question *What would happen if X situation could work as a Y situation?*, and this is particularly useful when we want to portray professions, personalities, famous people, relationships and even species we're not familiar with. We're getting a "map" from the situation from which we're borrowing the specifics.

Use what you have observed. Opinions and emotions are universal.

In general, initiating second beats requires precision. In particular, analogous second beats demand even more of that. Using the same lines of dialogue but with new specifics, emotions and movements, helps us make clear that we're rehashing the dynamic in a different universe.

The following ways to unify our set have to do with different games, that share common specifics:

Concept: Connections

Incorporating elements from previous scenes during a current one, merging the games.

Connections are likely to appear at the end of a set, like a "greatest hits" compilation.

A scene with connections looks like a second beat of two or more games within the same situation, by inserting in it either characters and/or dynamics previously seen during the set.

Furthermore, there's a place for an initiation that sets up from the beginning the connection between two or more scenes, calling the improvisers that are needed for that to take center stage.

There are shows that favor and even actively encourage that connections are explored. Connecting the dots is usually well received by the audience, given that it shows a little bit of mastery over our craft and it brings back characters and dynamics that were enjoyable; also, it makes the audience doubt if the piece was pre-written, which is the ultimate compliment for the improvisers.

Concept: Callback

Mentioning a specific from a previous scene during the current one.

This technique tends to be more shallow than connections, and involves mainly mentioning some detail that was previously displayed on the set. It can be from a situation or a character, to a thing or a concept.

Recovering concrete elements leaves us with the sensation of a shared universe, and the more specific they are, the more fun it is.

DISCOVER THE CONNECTIONS, DON'T FORCE THEM

Using both connections and callbacks should be done as long as it's organic, and not forced.

Bringing back characters that are incoherent with the situation has the opposite effect to the one we want to cause in the audience: the spectators see us inventing, making an effort and, to a certain point, desperate.

If I had a nickel for each callback that was unnecessary to play the game or to build a more solid reality... I could easily give up my day job and dedicate my entire life to improv, without any worries for the future at all.

Just as it's possible to have these isolated elements that go from one scene to the other, in the process of improvising we also can discover that the whole set has been unified by a deeper meaning.

Concept: Theme

Idea or concept that unconsciously has been a part
of most of the set.

Theme is among that series of ethereal and sort of
magical aspects of improv, and is probably the most
significant expression of **"group mind"** between those
who improvise together.

Whenever we've done some separate scenes, with
different games, and by the end we've figured out that all
of them were permeated by a big idea in general, it's like
we're in presence of a suggestion that time-traveled to
the beginning of our set, to inspire us.

Drawing the audience's attention to the apparition of the
theme is entirely optional; we could do a monologue
about it, create a scene that embodies it, or even keep
the satisfaction of having achieved it to ourselves.

IMPROVISING SUBTEXT

In other art forms, many times there's an intention by
the author of the piece to convey a specific message or
subtext that goes beyond the plot.

This elevates the scenic expression closer to what we
consider art.

> Improvising could make it possible to arrive at that level of bond with the audience, but with the magic of having found it with them as part of the journey.

· The structure of a set: Forms

Even though we have the scenic tools to give our set a sense of unity, we also can set up a defined structure in which we will pour our improvised scenes.

Counting on a pre-established shape to organize our show is still compatible with the spontaneous creation of the scenes. We're just putting them in a mold that doesn't significantly influence their content.

We refer to these structures as forms.

Concept: Form

A more or less pre-planned structure through which the scenes are presented.

Having a form gives us a sequence within which we can improvise, keeping the unity of the piece and generally favoring a show that's worthy of being watched.

Nowadays, a large variety of forms exists, and it's a number that will only grow with time. By analyzing what they have in common, most of them consist in three parts, with two of them being entirely optional:

- **Inspiration phase**. In this case, we're talking about the suggestion and/or an opening. As we've seen before, this is a phase that may be expendable.

- **Scenes**. This is the core part of our form, and it should encompass about 80 to 90% of the show.

Some aspects to define about this part, are:

- Are scenes related? How?
- Is there a specific order to follow?
- Is there a preferred number of cast members in each scene?
- How flexible is it to walk-on or to do tag-outs?
- Are we having another source of inspiration before the set ends?
- Do we have a "base scene" we're coming back to?
- Is there a specific way to edit?

Besides these questions, surely while designing your own form you'll find some more.

- **Closing the set**. Even though this isn't present in all forms, having a way to close gives us and the audience a sense of completing a scenic piece.

Said conclusion can be presentational or scenic. Presentational means addressing our audience directly, breaking the fourth wall as characters or as ourselves.

A scenic closing means ending the set with one or several scenes with some characteristics that distinguish them from the others, like the number of cast members, the presence of connections or theme, style, among others.

SOME FORMS TO EXPLORE

For this explanation to be less abstract, here's a list of some of the most popular forms with a brief description of their structure:

- **Harold**. It's the grandparent of all forms. In its more basic shape, it consists of an **opening** sparked by a **suggestion**, followed by the first beat of three scenes (and their games).

From there, comes a **group game** that isn't related to previous scenes and serves as a "palate cleanser" before starting a **second beat** of the same three scenes (in the same order), **following the game** of the original ones.

After that, a **second group game** takes place and to end the piece comes a **third beat**, where connections are desirable and the dynamics may or may not

---

coexist. Even more, it could be that instead of revisiting each game, all of them are contained within the same situation.

This form, by being so structured, contains many of the essential skills for those of us who improvise, which justifies what Matt Besser says about it: if we master the Harold, we'll easily adapt to the rest of the forms.

- **Montage**. The montage is a series of **unrelated scenes**. Just like that, this is one of the looser forms.

- **Armando**. The Armando is a **montage** that is preceded by a **monologue** presented by a player or a special guest, that should contain an anecdote and/or truthful opinion. The person presenting the monologue **can come back in the middle of the set** with another monologue, inspired by what happened in previous scenes.

Even though **connections** and **callbacks** aren't mandatory in this form, it's more than welcome in the end.

- **Living Room**. In this case, we make a **conversational opening**, and once the cast gets enough inspiration, they generate a scene or two. **By the end of them, we go back to the conversation** to obtain new inspiration for some more.

- **Slacker**. The name of this form comes from its fluid structure. After a **suggestion** and/or **opening**, a scene is initiated.

The participation via **support moves** by the rest of the team is welcome, but there are no **edits**. We just keep "following the fun" to new places, using a character or the other.

- **Pretty Flower / Spokane**. This is a form that has gained popularity in the last couple of years. After the **suggestion**, a **core, base or central scene** begins. When someone, be it a participant in the central scene or not, detects a comedic idea, they create a **tangential scene** inspired by that premise, to be explored and heightened.

When we've played enough of our tangent, it's edited by **going back to the base scene**, and this keeps happening throughout the form.

Depending on a previous agreement by the ensemble, our base will remain as if time didn't pass by during the tangential scene, or it could make a slight time dash.

- **La Ronde**. A great form for character development. In this one, beginning from a **suggestion** a **two-person scene** ensues, whom we'll call "A" and "B". By the end of the scene, **instead of editing**, "C" tags "A" out and starts a new one, where "B" **keeps their character and**

heightens it. Despite keeping a character present, we shouldn't follow their story, but a personality trait that becomes its game.

Likewise, to culminate this new scene, "D" tags "B" out while "C" remains and heightens, and so on **until the number of improvisers is exhausted** and the last person who started a scene, will share one with "A".

- **Monoscene**. This form usually has an **opening** by **scenepainting** or enters directly from an audience **suggestion** of a place.

Within the monoscene, several characters coexist **in only one location**, even though the **focus** is just in one part of them, and switches from relationship to relationship through entrances and exits. This form may have a structure like a **Harold** in one location, where **instead of tag-outs and beats there's a change of focus**.

- **Macroscene**. As an opposite of the monoscene, the macroscene **happens in several locations**, since its structure asks us to **follow a character that left the scene to create a new one**, which is repeated constantly.

- **Deconstruction**. Another very structured form is the deconstruction, which uses as an **opening** a **base**

scene with a realistic feel, with no need to make it funny, since it just serves as an inspiration for the rest.

From there **two scenes** follow, and they expose a couple of **themes** detected in the characters of our base; **we come back to the latter**, to then get to **five "commentary scenes"**, where we explore details about the original scene's characters.

Afterward, we return to that scene briefly, to then play a series of **short and fast scenes** mainly focused on **tangents and specifics**, giving way to the last **return** of the base scene that gives it a **conclusion**, which can be a time jump even to a point before we started our form. The base scene is informed by everything that happens in all of the other scenes.

I know. It sounds complex, but it's also fulfilling.

- **Close quarters**. This form, just like the **monoscene**, requires a **specific location** to work; and, especially, one that has many different spaces that are next to each other.

All scenes are observed separately, but they're happening at the same scenic time, even though they're in separate locations; so the audience is witness to the impact of events, sounds, entrances and exits in real time that impact all of the set.

- **The Documentary**. Perhaps one of the more structured and complex forms, created by Billy Merritt. After getting an event as a suggestion, improvisers face a made up camera by sitting down two by two and facing the audience.

After that, an improviser in the role of "the documentarian", states the themes and title of the fake movie, followed by character monologues and a flurry of both real and made up facts.

We then see actual scenes with the couples, but now without breaking the fourth wall. Next, we have a palate cleanser that may take one of many tropes of actual documentaries. After that we see another beat of the relationships, and a conclusion that involves following up those dynamics and an ending where the documentarian buttons up the piece.

The documentarian is free to go through scenes and comment or do interviews as they see fit.

- **Improvisaciones Mínimas**. Even though this isn't exactly a form that is played with game of the scene technique, it's an interesting contribution to check out since it's probably the most recognizable Latin American form.

Created by Sergio Lizzulli, a Peru based Argentinian teacher, it has basically this structure:

After an **organic opening**, comes the **first beat of two-person scenes**, followed by a **change of partner** in the same number of scenes, **keeping the same characters**.

By the end of that section, we'll introduce a **second beat of the initial scenes**.

At last, in the way I learned it, each character offers a **series of short monologues** toward the audience, and in the end all of them end up interlacing with one another.

Besides its structure, it's timely to say that "mínimas" carries that adjective ("minimal") because it pretends to show everyday lives, from a more stylistic than a structural point of view.

Like I said, the goal of this list is for you to see how different elements are manipulated to create a form that is distinct from the others. I invite you, if you want to delve deeper, to look for resources on the internet. There's a lot of information about them!

Creating a form of their own is an ambition of many improvisers while their career advances. Nevertheless, it should be clear: **A form will never be solid if the fundamentals of improv aren't consolidated**. Be sure to work on your basics before you explore complex structures that could blur the realities you want to create.

Same subject, but shorter:

Offer to the audience the sensation of an original and complete scenic piece.

Scene simulator

When we talk about support moves we showed a tag-out from our example scene, that could've worked as a second beat; so we'll observe how connections, callbacks and theme could work.

UNITING SCENES

(CONNECTION SCENE INITIATION)
A (From the "Shut up, I am posh" dynamic): "You see, actions have consequences. You and your wife went abroad, living fast and loose, but you're obviously not a Samantha"

(CALLBACK)
A: "Jail isn't so bad, newbie. Sometimes we jump over chairs to exercise just like they do in the Olympics"

(THEME MONOLOGUE)
A: (Toward the audience) "Everything you've seen so far is about holding back or going all in"

Workbook #6

Just for fun, create your own form. Establish which opening you would use (if you decide to have one),

how the scene structure would be and whether or not you'd incorporate a closing part.

Try not to overcomplicate your form. Design it having in mind that the audience should be able to follow it and enjoy it.

Appendix: Improvising online

I'm writing this book during the 2020/2021 pandemic. The day-to-day reality of everyone around the world changed in the way we live, work and relate to each other, and also the way we entertain and dedicate our time to our passions.

Those of us who improvise have this "yes, and" mentality embedded in how we see life. We accept the situation as real, we assimilate what we think or feel about it and we make choices accordingly.

We embraced several digital platforms to keep doing improv, and we adapted to the new conditions. I wanted to add this appendix to talk to you about some points to take into account about this medium.

---

1. Choices have to be made with even more clarity. Improvising from a distance limits the information that we can send to our counterpart. Body language loses a good chunk of its effectiveness and voice modulation is transmitted differently.

Because of that, expressing our ideas as concisely and accurately as possible is essential online; and this also entails conveying emotions so they can travel through the lens.

The other side of this coin is that...

2. We have to increase the intensity of the attention we imprint on our scenes. Del Close talked about being "paranoid" as an analogy of the magnitude that our state of alert should reach.

Let's capture the meaning of everything that happens and assign a subtext to the most minimal detail that we perceive to give emotional depth to our scenic creation and find its truth within itself.

3. Being more aware of taking turns and inhabiting silences. Internet connections are uneven in quality and they might cause unsyncing, freezing or image/sound distortions.

Because of that, breaking our "improviser rhythm" in which we answer almost immediately is more of a need than a style improvement.

4. Let's take advantage of the resources that online platforms have to offer. The evolution of improv helped itself by using technique shortcuts that allowed it to create on stage what normally happens in formal theater or a screen.

Scene transitions, the way we end them, the scenery, environment, "cinematography" and sound design, among many other conventions that we borrowed from the rest of the scenic arts, transformed our art form.

As the last century was winding down, The Family, a Chicago based improv team that was directed by Del Close, created The Movie, a form where movie genres were explored while the game was played. For a better effect, The Family found a way to portray different camera shots and movements, as well as a manner to narrate images that were impossible to create physically.

Back then, they needed to look for ways to communicate what a lens usually did; now, we have our mobile devices and computers that give us the opportunity to create cinematography. Experiment with it, with descriptions and narration, virtual backgrounds or green screens, sound effects and off-camera voices, and more.

Even further - and this is something that I don't especially enjoy in live improv - use objects around you to resignify them and enrich your reality.

5. We have the technique to present successful scenes. Let's adapt it to our circumstances. From the methods to get a suggestion and perform openings using our virtual environment, to the technique we use to incorporate support moves - or create new ones - let's put our creativity and the advantages that come with digital platforms to use.

6. Experiment. The forms I listed previously were created by improvisers that kept in mind the reality of a physical stage and proximity between players to innovate.

Organizing scenes in an ad hoc structure to the medium we choose - live video, recorded video, podcasts and those we can't even imagine - and managing their rhythm and cadence in a final product that is more enjoyable for virtual audiences, depends on a new generation of players.

I can't wait to see what else is coming.

What you found in this book
are concepts, tools and
techniques that are worthless
if they aren't practiced.

Also, if you're just
consuming, practicing,
and studying improv,
you're not experiencing.

Your experiences are what makes you
unique on and off-stage.

Live and play.

Read, listen and watch

Nowadays there's a lot of content available if you know where to look. Websites, books, podcasts and videos... all of them, important information sources at hand. Here are some recommendations.

Read

Books about long-form.

Truth in comedy
Del Close, Charna Halpern, Kim "Howard" Johnson

Upright Citizens Brigade comedy improvisation manual
Matt Besser, Ian Roberts, Matt Walsh

Improvising now: A practical guide to modern improv
Rob Norman

How to be the greatest improviser on earth
Will Hines

Del salto al vuelo (Spanish, but I'm pretty sure there's an English version)
Omar Argentino Galván

The triangle of the scene: A simple, practical, powerful method for approaching improvisation
Paul Vaillancourt

Pirate, Robot, Ninja: An improv fable
Billy Merritt, Will Hines

The complete improviser
Bill Arnett

Improvise: The scene from the inside out
Mick Napier

Improvisation at the speed of life
T.J. Jagodowski, David Pasquesi

Jill Bernard's small cute book of improv
Jill Bernard

This improv book
David Escobedo

Improv Nonsense (online blog)
Will Hines

r/improv subreddit
Reddit

Listen

Podcasts where long-form is played (the first two) and where theory is analyzed.

Improv 4 humans
Matt Besser

The meat improv
Jake Jabbour, Josh Simpson

The backline
Adam Cawley, Rob Norman

Improv beat by beat
Curtis Retherford

Professor Besser
Matt Besser

Improv Nerd
Jimmy Carrane

Exploring Improv
Andy Barrett

15 minutes of game
Matt Francis and Brian Hines

Long Form Short Pod (Bilingual Spanish and English)
Francisco Antillón (Shameless plug)

Some podcasts that aren't updated but have lots of good information: **Improv obsession podcast**, **IRC Podcast**, **Improv yak**, **UCB long-form conversations**, **The Pack Theater podcast**.

Watch

Video content where game-based long-form is practiced.

Upright Citizens Brigade ASSSSCAT!
YouTube

Upright Citizens Brigade - ASSSSCAT Improv
YouTube

Middleditch & Schwartz
Netflix

Do you have any questions or comments?
Send me an email at longformshortpod@gmail.com!

Printed in Great Britain
by Amazon